THE DREAM
LOVER

Les Peto has been involved in a wide range of
humanistic and transpersonal psychology group
work, and is a graduate of the facilitator training
programme of the Institute for the Development
of Human Potential (IDHP). He has also trained
with the Bath Individual Psychotherapy Group.
His private practice in Bristol makes use of a
wide range of techniques, including dreamwork,
imaging, and gestalt. He has also lectured and
broadcast on these subjects.

The computer-generated cover illustration is
based on an idea depicting the 'union of
irreconcilables', the marriage of water and fire.
The two figures each have four hands to signify
their many different capabilities (after an Indian
painting).

THE DREAM LOVER

Transforming Relationships Through Dreams

Les Peto

quantum

LONDON · NEW YORK · TORONTO · SYDNEY

quantum

An imprint of W. Foulsham & Co. Ltd.,
Yeovil Road, Slough, Berkshire SL1 4JH

ISBN 0–572–01583–6
Copyright © 1990 Les Peto

Printed in Great Britain at St Edmundsbury Press, Bury St Edmunds

CONTENTS

PREFACE

Beginning dreamwork is rather like pulling at a loose thread on a sweater — you never know how much will come out as you pull, and there is always the worrying thought that perhaps it's best left alone in case you inadvertently unravel the whole garment.

I first became curious enough to start pulling at the loose threads of my dreams twenty-five years ago, after reading Carl Jung's then newly-published book *Man and His Symbols*. I was particularly intrigued by his suggestion that I had an inner woman, my anima, ready to help and guide me in exploring the dark landscapes of my unconscious life, for at that time my outer relationships with women were often baffling and painful. I was ready to investigate any idea that promised to enhance my understanding of 'them', and solve the riddle of the opposite sex with its enigmatic mixture of intimacy and alienation.

I have been pulling out that particular thread for many years now and sure enough, in the process of developing a relationship with that inner woman, who I learned to call my Dream Lover, large parts of my personality *have* been unravelled, and re-knitted, several times. I realise now that I started out partly motivated by the chauvinistic notion that to know and understand women better would somehow eventually give me the knack of controlling and managing these unruly creatures more easily. I did not then fully understand that the thread of my dreams leads *inwards*, that it would involve me in a lengthy programme of self-exploration and development in many fields apart from dreamwork, and that my main task was to understand and accept the unruly alienated unknown feminine aspects of my *own* psyche.

Of course, the Dream Lover theme is not the only thread that will lead us into our dreams and into our unknown depths. Dreamwork can be centred on the symbols of a spiritual quest, or used to explore a creative path in one of the arts, and so on. Any of the dreamwork techniques presented in this book can readily be adapted to work on any .other theme that becomes important. Nevertheless, I recommend the Dream Lover as an entry point, not only because my extensive personal and professional work in this area has been richly rewarding, but also because the opposite sex offers an enduring symbol of the unknown, a constant challenge to learn more, go further, into the un-realised unconscious Self.

If you follow the thread offered by the Dream Lover, as outlined in this book, it will eventually lead you wherever you need to go, and over the years it will provide a satisfy-ing and creative theme for your self-development, no matter where you wander.

Twenty-five years after setting out to 'manage' the women in my life I now find myself in mid-life following the guidance of the Dream Lover as priestess of my inner church. So pull the thread by all means: this book will help you benefit from whatever comes out for you.

Les Peto

PART ONE
IDEAS

CHAPTER 1

I'LL SEE YOU IN MY DREAMS

INTRODUCING THE DREAM LOVER: The Inner Opposite
— Relating to the Dream Lover — Seeking Completion

INTRODUCING THE DREAM LOVER

I met a beautiful young man, dressed entirely in red. He smiled at me and silently took my hand. The shock of his touch ran up my arm and my whole body began to tingle. I was made of light, I was expanding. We floated upwards and then, to my delight, we were flying together. We flew effortlessly, hand in hand, over the sunlit landscape and on over the sea.

She led me up a metal ramp. It was a pedestrian bridge over a busy main road. In full view of the passersby she opened her fur coat to show me her nakedness. I was lying on my back as she straddled me, ready to make love. I was aroused and intensely anxious and embarrassed at the same time: it was so public. I remember staring at the silver pendant which hung between her breasts. One moment it was a cross, and then it changed to a pentacle, the sign of witch-craft.

He walked past the window in the moonlight. I was torn between curiosity — I wanted to shout and attract his attention — and dread. For I knew somehow that if he turned his face toward me it would be terrifying, like a zombie, with empty black eye-sockets, the living dead.

The girl on the muddy shore of the river was a poor orphan, over-worked and oppressed. My companions showed me what to do. They threw money to the girl. I was expected to do the same, to give her a fifty-pence piece. I felt awful. It was the only money I had. If I gave her my last coin I would be worse off than she was. I was in an agony of indecision. Guilt, anger and self-pity flowed through me.

11

The Dream Lover haunts the secret inner life of our dreams in a bewildering variety of forms. When we dream of the opposite sex, as illustrated in the above examples, we are likely to feel delighted, attracted, anxious and frustrated, just as we are in our real-life relationships.

I believe there are many connections between the two worlds; between experiences in the waking world and the inner world we visit whilst we sleep. In fact, dreams can be regarded as a magnifying mirror, reflecting everyday concerns. Hidden hopes, fears, prejudices and expectations are accurately reflected, but in a dramatised and often bizarre form. So whenever the Dream Lover appears in the mirror, he or she is usually much larger than life.

But who, or what, *is* the Dream Lover?

The Inner Opposite

I have chosen this term primarily to describe opposite sex figures in dreams, but it also refers to the source of such dreams, which lies within the dreamer. Every woman carries within her an image of 'Man', and every man has a complementary inner image of 'Woman'. These are the basic blue-prints of the Dream Lover.

When a woman dreams of a male figure, she creates him through unconscious reference to her inner male image, which she has built up and constantly modified since she was born. He is the sum total of all she has experienced, read about, seen or been told about the male sex. He also represents, and enables her to dis-associate from, the more 'masculine' aspects of her own personality which are likely to remain largely latent — unless they are evoked by some crisis — until she reaches mid-life.

A man who dreams of a woman will go through a similar process; the figure in his dream will be a reflection of his relationship to his inner 'feminine' side, which again is likely to remain unacknowledged and undeveloped in his conscious personality until later life.

12

Many psychologists have adopted Prof. C.G. Jung's system of naming a woman's inner male potential her 'animus', and a man's inner woman his 'anima', but I find in practice that these terms are generally unfamiliar and obscure to most people not directly involved in the field of psychology. I therefore propose instead to use the term Dream Lover throughout this book, as offering a more vivid, unisex name for the opposite gender elements we all contain, and which are constantly featured in dreams.

As we shall see, the Dream Lover presents us with an endless variety of forms — good, bad, commonplace and strange — for our inner 'other half' is just as complex, confusing, mysterious and fascinating as the opposite sex is in real life.

Whether or not we choose to develop this latent side of our personalities, it exists, and real-life relationships can be unconsciously shaped and coloured by our relationship with our Dream Lover. Whilst we sleep, this other half takes on a whole repertoire of roles, from star to bit-player, in the never-ending drama of dreams. If we are willing we can tune in to this process and learn of new parts of our total self.

Relating to the Dream Lover

Considering the average person's preoccupation with relationships and the enormous influence these have on the quality of our lives, it is not surprising that this forms a major theme in our dreamlife.

What *is* surprising is how rarely it occurs to us to record and study dreams of the opposite sex. Yet these can form the basis of an exciting and rewarding new relationship, with the Dream Lover. In developing this relationship we can gain much personal insight and understanding in dealings with the partners we have in real-life, as well as embarking on a challenging new period of growth for ourselves.

This book will show you how to meet and get to know your Dream Lover in a constructive way. In the process, we will be taking a close look at where he or she came from, seeking the root models and experiences, often in early childhood, which originally formed our ideas and assumptions about the opposite sex.

My purpose is to provide you with some useful 'programme notes' to help you explore and understand the dramas of your inner and outer relationships. But I cannot tell you what the plot will be. We are all writing our own private stories about the Dream Lover, and as you will discover in later chapters, only the dreamer can ever fully understand the images in the dream.

One thing I can promise: when you start to work on your dreams there will be no shortage of material. Scientists have shown that everyone dreams several times every night. Every ninety minutes or so, throughout the night, we have a spell of dreaming. Provided that you have a normal sleep of eight hours, therefore, you will have treated yourself to at least five gripping episodes of this long-running inner serial. Usually, however, we only remember the last one or two dream stories that occur just before waking.

Despite these facts, many people claim that they never dream, except perhaps for the occasional nightmare, which is usually dismissed as 'something I ate' and then forgotten as quickly as possible. I think it would be more accurate for such people to say 'I won't remember my dreams,' rather than, 'I can't remember my dreams.' If we consciously choose to ignore or dismiss our dreams as meaningless it is not surprising that we will then pay no attention to the swiftly fading memories and feelings of our latest dreams as we emerge from sleep.

Yet why should we choose to ignore our dreams, to turn away from what Freud called the 'Royal Road to the unconscious'? Let's face it: the process of looking within can be difficult and painful sometimes, as well as exciting and rewarding. There will always be some degree of hesitation

14

and resistance when we approach something unknown or unacknowledged in ourselves.

The subject we are about to focus on will also produce its own difficulties, even though it is an important and interesting endeavour. Inevitably, the process of looking at the Dream Lover will bring up many memories, not all of them pleasant, for most of us have much unfinished business resulting from our life-long interactions with the opposite sex.

For those who do experience difficulties in remembering dreams, therefore, I have suggested various simple methods of encouraging recall in Chapter 3.

Seeking Completion

It is only when we begin to study our dreams in general that we realise the central importance of the Dream Lover. The majority of dreams contain some reference to the opposite sex. He may be centre-stage, the focus of the dream, or she may appear almost like an 'extra' on the edges of the main story: 'As I ran, my legs turned to jelly. I struggled on down the road, frightened to look back. I passed *a woman looking at dresses* in a shop window, and then, at the end of the street . . .'

The all-pervading presence of our opposites in our dreams is likely to be one of the first things you notice when you start to keep a dream diary.

This is hardly surprising, for dreams faithfully reflect everyday concerns, and most people are preoccupied to some degree with their relations to the opposite sex throughout life. Variations on the theme are: how to meet, select, approach, join, avoid, live with, or get away from our 'other half'.

Underlying the more obvious motivations such as sexual and emotional needs, and the desire to raise a family, there is another almost wistful, yet powerful desire. This is often expressed to me as a feeling of being somehow incomplete or stuck, unable to move without the 'right relationships'. In my counselling work a man may say, 'Until I meet the right woman I feel I can't concentrate on work or anything else. What's the point?' Or a woman might say, 'The rest of my life seems meaningless without him.'

In this book I am suggesting that we can make valuable progress towards satisfying the need for a feeling of wholeness, by turning part of our attention inwards. The Dream Lover can help in surprising ways in this quest.

The man who has achieved some degree of peace and harmony with his inner woman is more likely to respect and appreciate the qualities of the women he meets in reality. And a woman who has similarly come to terms with her inner man is likely to feel more balanced and confident in her dealings with men. It is obvious that such an increase in mutual understanding helps remove some of the conflict in relationships, releasing more energy for creative and enjoyable interplay between us.

But whether you are seeking inner wisdom from your Dream Lover, or whether you are more interested in gaining insights about your current relationships, the first step will be to learn, or rather remember, the symbolic language of your own dreams, and this forms the subject of the next chapter.

CHAPTER 2

THE FORGOTTEN
LANGUAGE

---

*UNDERSTANDING DREAM SYMBOLS: The Feeling-Picture
Show — Meet the Author — Too Clever by Half —
The Cultural Context — The Personal Context*

UNDERSTANDING DREAM
SYMBOLS

If the Dream Lover is to become more than just a passing
stranger in our lives we need to find ways of opening up a
dialogue.

In a sense the problem resembles the dilemma that would
face us if we met an interesting foreigner whose language
was a mystery to us. In our eagerness to overcome the
language barrier as quickly as possible we might struggle
with an inadequate phrase book, or perhaps take along an
interpreter. But if we really want to develop a deeper mutual understanding, starting to learn the new language for
ourselves is the soundest approach.

There are 'phrase books' — dream dictionaries — on the
market, containing alphabetical lists of symbols together
with their 'meanings'. Looking up your dream in such a
dictionary, as you may have discovered, can be a frustrating
experience.

In the first place you may find that the image you have

17

dreamed is not listed. This is almost inevitable, because the creative variety of dream content is literally infinite, and we frequently 'dream up' people, objects and situations which simply do not exist in the real world. Another drawback is that, assuming the symbol you are interested in is listed, you may find that the interpretation given doesn't help much in understanding your particular dream as a whole.

You may for example find that a hat is said to represent mental attitudes and conscious intentions. But let's say that the head-gear worn by the fascinating stranger in last night's dream was a turban, made of green garden netting, and that he was busy pouring champagne onto the floor . . .?

Clearly, a list of symbols with predetermined meanings attached is likely to be of limited use to anyone wanting more than a superficial understanding of their dreams. The generalised explanations often don't feel right, and the acid test of any interpretation of a dream symbol is whether it rings true for the dreamer.

As an alternative to the phrase-book approach, we could take our dreams to a 'translator'. It is possible, for example, to consult a professional psychotherapist in this regard, although generally speaking dreamwork on this level is more appropriate for someone who is deeply committed to a much wider programme of self-development. At the other extreme you might find someone among your friends who shares your interest. Most people enjoy relating their dreams, and comparing experiences with a sympathetic friend can be helpful in focusing on the thoughts, feelings and memories sparked off by the dream.

However, this book is written primarily for the do-it-yourself dream interpreter. I recommend that you try out all the various techniques and exercises mentioned in later chapters and stay with the ones that work best for you.

This new skill that you are learning is much more an art than a science. So let us now forget any ideas about obtaining ready-made answers from phrase-books or other people.

You are the only person who will ever be able to fully understand the private language of your own dreams, and you will automatically develop this skill in the process of pursuing the Dream Lover.

As I have hinted before, the task is not so much to learn anew but to remember what has been forgotten. And you can start to jog your memory by first looking more closely at the form in which the dream experience comes.

The Feeling-Picture Show

Dreams are primarily 'feeling-pictures'. They are almost entirely silent movies, and rely for their impact on striking, often brightly coloured, visual images. Frequent use is made of larger than life, surreal and irrational situations.

Dialogue is used much more sparingly than in real life; when spoken or written words appear in the dream they are often highly significant, and should be given special attention. Typically, these words and phrases are Sphinx-like in nature, sometimes delivered in a 'God-like' voice from above', and leaving us with further riddles to solve.

In complete contrast to the emotional picture language of dreams, the waking self is usually busy translating impulses and experiences into words, logic and intellectual understanding. While the dreaming mind produces 'films', the waking, rational mind produces 'newspapers'.

Although one picture may be worth a thousand words, most of us are convinced that we need the words too, in order really to grasp the meaning. Faced with an avant-garde film, or an experimental television feature, it is hard to resist the reassurance of turning to the programme notes or the critic's review; someone else will use words to tell us who wrote it and why, what it is about, and what it *means*. But learning the language of dreams involves developing one's own faculty for translating pictures into words, and for telling ourselves what the images mean.

Acknowledging the essentially pictorial nature of dreams

is in fact the first step towards understanding their messages. To illustrate this point, let us pretend that you are a brilliant film director with a reputation for making deeply meaningful 'art movies'. You plan to create a five-minute silent movie, and the story you want to put across concerns the plight of a man who was jilted by the woman he loved, and consequently became defensive and withdrawn. He avoids further hurt by hiding his feelings and warily keeping his distance from women.

Without the use of words, how would the director set about getting the 'picture' across to the audience? One approach would be to make our hero's costume symbolise his inner feelings. Perhaps we could start with the image of a man in a suit of armour. To add to the drama we might introduce a woman into the plot. We could show her trying to embrace the man — without much satisfaction! — and then, with a frown, taking up a bow and firing an arrow at the man's steel breast-plate, where it glances off harmlessly.

Now comes a quick change of scene to the armoured man's residence. We choose to have him live at the top of an isolated tower, without any windows, and which is entered through a secret door, because this again provides a simple yet effective way to portray the character's emotional position.

Taking off his armour, he reveals a tee-shirt with a large red heart printed on the front. The heart is pierced by an arrow. The man removes the tee-shirt and folds it carefully into a large, leather-covered diary which he places in a steel safe. Through the open door of the safe we glimpse other symbols of objects that he has locked away in the past: a bunch of rusty keys (unused because he never intends to open up again), a dead sea-gull (the spirit of his freedom), a tress of his former lover's hair fashioned into a noose . . .

Our imaginary silent film, relying heavily for its impact on symbolic images and melodramatic mime rather than dialogue, already begins to resemble a typical dream, does it not? Indeed, you will have noticed in the cinema that dream sequences, fantasies and sometimes 'flash-backs' are conventionally presented in slow-motion and in silence. At most, the sound-track will carry eerie music or perhaps the rhythmic thud of a heart-beat to help heighten the emotional tension.

Meet the Author

Having realised how closely dreams resemble short, silent movies, the second important point to understand is that we write the scripts ourselves. We also choose all the actors, all the props and locations, to illustrate our selected themes. The resultant dream movie is privately screened for just one privileged spectator: each of us is his or her own exclusive audience, too.

An astonishing amount of creativity is involved in this process. Everyone is a dramatic genius when it comes to filling the night-time screen with exciting and significant stories. When you begin to write your dream diary, notice how tirelessly the dream genius works to create these productions. Snippets gathered from a magazine, a character from a show you saw on TV, an unusual house you noticed as you passed in your car, a man in the queue in the local shop — all sorts of impressions are gathered and stored, ready to be skilfully included in a forthcoming dream.

The range of material that the dreamer calls on is boundless. You may find images from the past: a meeting with a long-forgotten playmate from primary school, the lady in the corner shop near your childhood home. Or from the future: the dreamer can visit strange planets, encounter alien life-forms, take part in Star Wars. Characters from fiction and history, pop stars, your dentist, the Royal Family — anyone and anything can be woven into your personal story if it suits you. There are no budget limitations to worry about in the dream cinema.

Too Clever by Half

An often overlooked fact is that we do not have to learn how to do all this. We automatically possess, we are apparently born with, the dramatic skill, creative flair and deep understanding of symbolism to produce dreams effortlessly, night after night.

What is puzzling is what happens to this natural fluency and understanding when we wake up? How is it that we are usually baffled when we try to unravel the meanings of our own creations in the light of day?

I believe that a major handicap to this understanding is that we try to be too clever by half when we sit down to interpret the dream. If we want to understand the foreigner, remember, we must be open to his way of expressing himself, in feeling-picture language. Only after we have received these simple, obvious messages can we translate and elaborate them into our familiar waking terms of words and logic.

The emotional, pictorial form of the dream closely resembles the intense and lucid experience of childhood. Most of us recall those early years in a series of simple, vivid and emotionally rich visual impressions. So, as we start to work more closely with the language of symbols it helps if we can cultivate a childlike simplicity in our approach. The adult mind, the clever bit, will be all too ready to supply complicated commentaries and footnotes later. After all, making up dreams is as easy as childsplay; perhaps interpretation is just as easy once we put aside our cleverness and stick to the obvious.

In childhood, we have the magic ability to talk to objects and animals, and to turn one thing into another, because originally we experienced few fixed boundaries between the imagination and external reality. By remembering how easy and familiar we used to be with this magical interplay, we can start to broaden the present ability to understand dreams.

When I was a child the tin kettle simmering on the hob really did sing. It was a cheerful, contented and comforting fellow, and the singing was part of its character. I had no reason to analyse my relationship with the kettle, it never occurred to me to question its personality: it simply *had* a personality, and I automatically understood what it was. Had I felt inclined to, I could have asked it about itself, and intuitively received answers.

I had the same sort of live and meaningful relationship with my toys. Using my lead soldiers, model animals and dolls as 'real' characters, I wove endless stories for my own amusement (and learning). In those days, too, I assume that the gap between my sleeping dreams and my waking play was not as wide as it now is.

Despite our cultural training towards rational, straight-line thinking, the magical world of the imagination remains largely intact, and playing with 'feeling-pictures' at second hand, through the cinema and television, continues to give enjoyment throughout life. We can take the same pleasure, at first hand, through 'playing' with our dreams.

The Cultural Context

This childhood faculty for projecting imagination onto the real world is not buried as deeply as you may think. We can dig it out and start using it to understand dreams quite easily. For instance, your car has a personality, has it not? Your house has its own character?

If I were to mention any common animal, you would be able to describe its character instantly, without having to figure out its 'meaning'. You just know that snakes are treacherous, foxes are cunning, pigs are greedy, horses are patient and hardworking, dogs are loyal, doves are peaceful, elephants never forget, owls are wise, monkeys are mischievous, and so on. Does the sea have emotions? Apparently, for even the most rational and level-headed adult has no trouble in understanding that the sea can be raging, calm, threatening, cruel, playful.

What about the Good Fairy? How does she look? The answers are easy: smiling, dressed in white, twinkling with points of light, long blonde hair. Yet, when we meet a blonde, smiling woman in a dream, dressed in sparkling white, we are bemused . . . how can we possibly work out what part of our personality *she* represents?

These examples reflect a common cultural background, as we share a kind of symbolic infra-structure which has been garnered from nursery rhymes, fairy stories, *Aesop's Fables*, *The Jungle Book*, and so on. We are never likely to confuse the Good Fairy with the Bad Fairy because we all know that the bad one wears cob-webby black shawls, has grey hair and a permanently ill-tempered expression. When I was a boy it was a standard cliché in the Saturday matinée cowboy serials that the goodies always wore white hats and the baddies wore black.

Clearly, we share a great deal of background knowledge which enables the making of instant interpretations of common symbols. In effect we already own an internal dream dictionary, and a moment's reflection will usually give us a ready-made meaning for many images.

However, in all the examples I have mentioned — the animals, the characters from childhood stories — it is assumed that the *common* interpretation applies to everyone's experience. But of course it doesn't.

The Personal Context

Nine out of ten people might agree that snakes are, indeed, treacherous. But what about the woman who had a harmless snake as a pet when she was a child? She will 'just know' that snakes are warm and friendly companions. And the toddler who has been bitten by a dog may well grow up knowing intuitively that dogs, although they may pretend to be affectionate, are basically vicious and not to be trusted.

This is what I mean by saying that only the dreamer can fully understand the true meaning of the dream. Your task involves discovering what the symbols you choose mean for you alone. To achieve this you need to go beyond clichéd interpretations and cultural stereotypes and put each dream firmly into the context of your personal experience.

A woman once told me a dream in which she discovered a large black spider sitting on the snowy white cover of her bed. Immediately, my mind started jumping to conclusions: women are frightened of spiders, therefore this was a frightening dream. The virginal white bed? Obviously she felt fear and conflict in her sexual relationships. I didn't voice these instant assumptions, however, but instead asked her what she felt about spiders. *Not* fear, it turned out, but friendly respect. 'I think of spiders', she said, 'as friendly visitors from another world, a world that is a mystery for me.'

What actually concerned her was that the spider on the bed was out of place — highly visible and out in the light. 'Their natural world is dark and secretive. Why should a spider come out into the light?' She was puzzled, not frightened, and as we worked together she gradually resolved the mystery to her own satisfaction.

The secret world of darkness and mystery represented her deep personal interest in astrology and the tarot cards. There had been some difficulty for her in bringing her dark talents out into the light of the practical world, and the dream helped her focus on her hesitation about taking the bold step of trying to make a living from astrology.

The personal context is absolutely vital in understanding the dream. Taken out of this context the dream could mean anything or nothing; it *only* has meaning for the dreamer. With this in mind let's examine another sample dream:

> I had been given a baby to look after. Time passed, and the mother didn't return. I was really annoyed. I'd been lumbered with a baby that didn't belong to me, and now I'd be stuck with it for the rest of my life. Then Bill came along and offered to

help. I put the baby into his arms and he went out somewhere. I felt relieved but also guilty. Supposing the mother returned now? I had no idea where her baby had been taken. I woke up feeling awful and confused. For a minute or two I couldn't be sure whether or not I *did* have a real child to care for.

What does this dream mean? Taken in isolation, without the context of the dreamer's life, it means nothing beyond the factual information it contains. But as you read it, you will have unconsciously 'tried it on for size', putting it into your own personal context, because we just cannot bear to hear a story without knowing its meaning. If we don't know the dreamer's personal background we will supply our own.

Whatever the above dream means to the individual reader is true for that person, but only that person. What you are in fact doing is running the story through your personal computer with the question: 'If this were *my* dream, what would it be about?'

In the case of a male reader, the answer would depend on whether he was a father, or maybe an expectant father. Who is Bill in this man's life? An older and perhaps more responsible brother? If the dreamer were a woman the dream might reflect her mixed feelings about her role as mother, or mother to be. The dreamer's age and general life situation would also strongly colour the message of the dream, giving it unique, personal shades of meaning.

The real dreamer in the above example was, in fact, a woman in her thirties, with two teenage children. She was medically unable to have further babies. Bill was her current partner, and it quickly emerged that the 'baby' which she passed to him represented a joint professional venture that they planned (conceived) together. Her dream was telling her that although she consciously blamed him for holding up the project through lack of commitment, she was also quite ready to dump all the responsibility into his lap. Let him be left 'holding the baby' if their new infant venture failed to get off the ground. She felt guilty because although in fact she was a parent to the plan, she didn't want to acknowledge it: the 'real mother' in the dream was 'someone else'. And behind the guilt lurked her resentment and fear that she was about to be lumbered with the entire responsibility for nurturing their joint plan.

So we can see that, although we approach the dream with a wide 'common knowledge' of what things mean, our personal knowledge adds crucial information to a full understanding.

In this book we shall focus our attention on a particular kind of dream, in which the Dream Lover appears in various symbolic guises. General knowledge of the opposite sex will give many clues to meaning, although we must beware of settling for stereotyped explanations — not everyone wearing a black hat is a bad guy. Our personal context for looking at these dreams will be our individual experiences with the real, unique men and women in our lives. Potentially, therefore, you have access to all the answers you need to help you use the Dream Lover to understand and develop your relationships more fully.

The only key you will need to unlock the answers is the right question. A large part of dreamwork, whether one is working alone or with someone else, consists of asking the right questions of the dreamer. That is why I shall be suggesting a great many questions and lines of self-enquiry in the chapters ahead. Inevitably, the sample dreams I use to illustrate each topic will always belong to someone else, but they will help you learn to apply self-questioning systematically to your own dreams.

First, though, it is necessary to start recording the raw material in a dream diary.

CHAPTER 3

DEAR DIARY

*HOW TO RECORD YOUR DREAMS: Eye-witness Accounts
— How Did It Feel? — Keeping the Dream Alive —
The Detached Point of View — Resisting the Dream*

HOW TO RECORD YOUR DREAMS

If you rely entirely on memory to recall your dreams, you will have little chance to study them systematically. Most dreams fade rapidly, like water into sand, within minutes of waking.

By keeping a dream diary not only are the fleeting images captured in permanent form, but the first big step is also taken in the task of translating pictures into words. By recording the curious silent movies of dreams in writing, they are immediately brought closer to everyday understanding.

I recommend that you keep pencil and paper handy by the bed, so that you don't lose precious minutes hunting for them when you waken. A loose-leaf folder is a practical way of storing your dreams, for it allows you to add pages of comment later. It is also useful to be able to take out scattered examples of recurring dream symbols and study them as a complete pattern or series.

Record all your dreams. Don't wait for a 'good' relationship dream to arrive. The Dream Lover may not appear for a time, but meanwhile you are developing the habit of accurate and systematic recording. You are also consciously opening the door to your dreamworld and inviting this unfamiliar side of your nature to develop. When dreams involving the opposite sex do appear, put them aside for use in your work with this book, but keep an eye on the general picture. At a later date you might want to go back over your dream diary and work on other kinds of dreams that frequently occur.

Eye-witness Accounts

When you come to describe the scene you have just witnessed in your dream, try to develop the novelist's eye for telling detail as well as the reporter's record of the bare facts.

For the purpose of this book we want to gather as complete a picture of the Dream Lover as possible. So notice and record details that will help you understand his or her character — age, height and weight for example. Clothing: style and colours. Physical condition: illness, injury or deformity. Hair and eye colour. Body language: gestures, facial expressions. Does the Dream Lover appear as a stranger, or is it someone you know, or knew in the past? Does he want to give you something, or take something from you? Is she a threat or a promise?

Don't overlook the setting of the dream, for the context colours the message. How and where did you meet the Dream Lover? Upstairs, downstairs, in a building or in a landscape? In daylight or darkness, winter or summer?

In what sort of house, in what sort of room does the meeting take place? Obviously, an exciting rendezvous in a pink boudoir at the top of a palace conveys quite a different message from a panicky encounter in the cellar of a dark castle. Dallying with a youth in a sunlit glade is one thing, whereas grappling with the same person on the edge of a cliff during a raging storm is another! Perhaps these examples seem self-evident, but it is surprising how often a person will become too focused on the figure to even remember the background.

How Did It Feel?

Note down any feelings, positive or negative, that you experienced during the dream. What we feel about somebody is, in dreamwork as in real life, much more powerful in guiding our actions than our thoughts about the person. We may believe that we evaluate and make choices quite rationally, while in truth we are often swayed by unconscious feelings of attraction or repulsion. In dreams, hidden emotions are much more 'up front' and accessible, so take the opportunity to record and learn from them, even if they don't make sense at first sight.

Keep an eye open for simple figures of speech which might be overlooked because they come in pictorial form. Having dreamed of thrusting a struggling cat into a paper bag, it may dawn on you *as you write it down* that you are anxious not to reveal some secret — not to let the cat out of the bag. Similarly, a dream may tell you that you fear 'spilling the beans' in front of your lover; that you think of him as a 'stick in the mud', or that he's 'hiding his light under a bushel', and so on. A puzzling scene often translates simply into one of these plays on words that can be readily understood.

Keeping the Dream Alive

Record the dream in the present tense, as if it were happening as you write your account: 'I am climbing a rickety ladder into the apple tree, looking up at this man in the top branches. My eyes are focused on the strange shoes he is wearing . . . I'm feeling curious and slightly at risk now . . .' This simple recording technique helps enormously to bring the dream back to life when you re-read it later. The here-and-now language reminds you of what it *felt* like to be in this dream.

Having recorded your dream, pause for a moment and see if you can write down the theme of the dream: 'avoiding danger', 'getting lost', 'anxious about being late'. Then give the dream a title, as if it were a little story: 'Jane Misses the Bus', 'John Comes to Tea', 'How I Killed the President', 'The Escaping Lion'. Don't spend too much time pondering on exactly the right theme or title for the dream; just write down your first thoughts. When you return to the dream to work on it more thoroughly, these first impressions, written down whilst the dream is still vivid in your memory, will often prove to be uncannily accurate pointers to the key message of the dream.

You may also feel like drawing a simple sketch of any particularly unusual dream person or object. Having a picture in front of you may help you notice important details of dress, shape, colour or size when you study it later.

The Detached Point of View

For many of us it is so much easier to see the wood when the trees happen to belong to someone else! When our friends get lost among the complexities of their relationship problems, we seem to be able to draw on a wealth of sympathetic understanding, clarity and simple solutions to help them out. We can see the broad picture, go to the heart of the matter, because we can be more detached about the problem.

This same principle applies to dreamwork. We can cultivate a more objective point of view by using the perspective of time. When you start to record and work with your dreams, you are likely to feel overwhelmed by the amount of material you gather. A practical way of handling this problem is to adopt the following schedule:

1 Record all your dreams, using the methods I have described.

2 At the end of each week, look back over your diary and select one 'star' dream.

3 Work on this one dream for the whole of the following week.

In this way you will aways be working in arrears; you come back to the dream a week later, hopefully with more detachment and with the wisdom of hindsight. As your skill develops you will be able to look at more dreams more quickly, with an increasingly objective and accurate understanding.

Don't forget to date each dream. Over a period of months or years you will be able to see that certain symbols and situations recur, and accurate dating can be helpful in relating these dream patterns to the rhythm of waking life. You may, for example, notice that similar types of dreams occur regularly at certain times of year, or that your dream pattern changes at the weekend. You may find that your dreams are significantly different while on holiday, compared with those you have throughout the working year, or that special dreams appear around the anniversary of your marriage, divorce, a bereavement or a birthday, and women may discover that certain images recur regularly with their menstrual cycle.

Resisting the Dream

By deciding to take dreams seriously and to look at them systematically, we open a door to unknown parts of ourselves. What comes through the door depends in part on how much we really trust the process. The first thing that comes may be — nothing! Formerly prolific dreamers may dry up completely for a while, pencil poised, book in hand, and nothing to work on.

What does this mean? I would suggest that 'no dream' is a message in itself, telling us that we are not entirely ready to plunge into unfamiliar territory. On some level we still have reservations about acknowledging that dreams play an important part in our lives, or perhaps we fear looking too closely at ourselves in case something nasty emerges.

Alternatively, you may find that you dream just as frequently as before, but that since opening this book you dream of every conceivable subject except the opposite sex. Your conscious intention of focusing on the Dream Lover may be, at least temporarily, out-weighed by your resistance to letting a lot of troublesome skeletons out of the cupboard.

There are various ways of priming the pump, to encourage an easier flow of dreams, but remember that if you really don't want to know there is no point in trying to force the process. As a temporary measure, you could use a ritual just before you drop off to sleep each night, telling yourself, 'Tonight I feel like having a dream, and I will remember it in the morning.' You can also write the words, 'What was the dream?' on a piece of card, and prop it up on the bedside table so that you prompt yourself to remember as soon as you wake up. Then, allow yourself a few minutes to relax and become aware of any feelings that you have woken with. Recontacting the feelings often encourages images to float back into consciousness and the dream memory may follow.

A sense of relaxed openness to the natural flow of your dreams is the best way to encourage and deepen your dreamwork. This book presupposes that you want to focus your work on exploring the Dream Lover, either because you want to widen your personality through developing the inner man or woman, or because you want to improve your relationships. But whatever their frequency and whatever their subject, you can be certain that the dreams you are having now are the important ones for you. Don't try to compel yourself to produce the right kind of dream. Whenever you are ready, the Dream Lover will start to appear.

Meanwhile, any dream you have is the right dream for you now.

PART TWO
EXPLORATION

CHAPTER 4

INTO THE MAZE

*MAPPING THE RELATIONSHIP: An Introduction to
Part Two*

MAPPING THE RELATIONSHIP

Having read and absorbed the ideas in the first part of this book, and with personal material about the Dream Lover beginning to accumulate in your dream diary, you are now ready to start out on the exploration of your relationship with your other half, represented by the opposite sex in real life, and by the Dream Lover in your dreams.

But where should one begin? In many ways, involvements with the opposite sex resemble a maze. We proceed by trial and error, take many wrong turnings, and rarely have a clear picture of our overall situation — or indeed of the ultimate objective of our quest — and when we begin to explore the unconscious side of our lives reflected in our dreams, we are even more at a loss about how to proceed.

What is needed in both cases is a map, and in Part Two I have set out some of the main landmarks and turning points that might be encountered during the course of a typical relationship.

Involvements with the opposite sex tend to follow a classic sequence of recognisable stages. We acknowledge these patterns when we find ourselves using clichés to describe the progress of our own, or our friends' affairs:

'They're still going through the honeymoon phase,' we say, or 'I hear John and Jane are on the rocks again.' I have made use of many of these common expressions as chapter headings in the following section, because they are so universally understood.

A broad outline, a sketch map if you like, of a typical relationship would look something like this: starting with an initial attraction, it progresses through increasing intimacy to a sexual stage, and then enters a honeymoon phase. After the honeymoon, when everything, hopefully, will have been wonderful, doubts, criticisms and resentments begin to emerge, clouding the shining image we have of our new partners.

This middle phase, which may form the major part of the relationship, is all about conflict and co-operation, compromise, values, negotiation, discussion, sharing — in short coming to terms with the problems thrown up by two separate and unique individuals working out how best to live closely together. During this phase, self-knowledge is important, because we need to find our own honest answers to such questions as, 'What do I want from this relationship? What am I prepared to give? How far will I compromise my own values? Am I willing to alter my personal priorities and set different goals?'

The ability to communicate and negotiate with our partners is always an important factor in maintaining satisfying relationships, but during the middle phase the willingness to talk openly and honestly is crucial.

Often, too, relationships are tested to breaking point by the appearance of a rival, real or imagined. The 'other woman' or the 'other man' may compete with you for the affections of your lover, or perhaps the relationship will become strained because of your own growing interest in someone else. Whatever the cause, such events are likely to arouse deep-seated issues concerning your personal security and self-worth.

Ultimately, a crisis of choice emerges. Both partners have

to decide whether to commit themselves to a long-term relationship — marriage and a family perhaps — or whether to end the affair.

In this respect the Dream Lover, because of its internal nature, is unique, for we are all already committed to a life-long relationship with this inner partner. Despite the variety of guises adopted by the Dream Lover and despite all the ups and downs, satisfactions and difficulties it presents, we cannot ever separate completely, for it is truly part of ourselves.

In the following eight chapters we will cover much of this ground by focusing on particular topics that arise in relationships, exploring some of the problems involved and some of the lessons to be learned. I will also try to illustrate how real-life situations can be reflected in your experiences with the Dream Lover, by presenting particular kinds of opposite sex dreams, such as sexual dreams and nightmares. The overall aim will be to help you to establish a two-way flow of sharper self-awareness and creative insight between your inner self and your outer partners.

To enable you to work quickly and effectively on this exploratory process, I will show you how to use modern dreamwork techniques to unravel the mysteries of your own Dream Lover, and point out ways in which you can relate this new knowledge to real-life situations.

Throughout this section I will present examples of typical Dream Lover sequences, taken from the dreams of men and women of all ages. These examples are used to show in closer detail how to put the dreamwork exercises into action for yourself.

I hope you will also use Part Two as an opportunity to review the history of your own present and past relationships. You may be able to identify how successful you are at handling some stages of a relationship, and how unsuccessful you are at negotiating other stages. It may be that things always go wrong for you when the honeymoon is over, or you may discover you have a repetitive pattern of jealousy.

You might also like to use these chapters to help you ponder over a current relationship: what stage would you say you've reached with this particular partner, and what sort of dreams are you now having?

Remember that when you are lost in a maze, it doesn't immediately solve the problem to know where you are now, but it's certainly a helpful start.

CHAPTER 5
AT FIRST SIGHT

DREAMS ABOUT STRANGERS: The Unconscious Computer
— Blind Dates in Dreams — Association Exercise —
John's Story

DREAMS ABOUT STRANGERS

All relationships start with a first impression. And many finish right there, with that same initial response.

Is there such a thing as love at first sight? Many people believe so, and many have experienced the surprise, delight and panic at being more or less overwhelmed by a sudden and intense interest in a man or woman they have only just met. Many people, too, have experienced the opposite response, with equally intense feelings of dislike, even revulsion, after a brief encounter.

The more normal response to meeting a stranger of the opposite sex is less passionate and more a question of interest or lack of interest, curiosity or boredom.

However intense or moderate one's response, what is actually going on during the crucial first few seconds or minutes of the new acquaintance? Clearly, we must at some level be picking up clues, gathering data, evaluating this, and coming up with a judgement: 'I think I might like this man,' or 'I think I'll have another look round, this man's a bore.' What are the important factors that lead to these conclusions?

In real-life, as in dreams, I believe that the *visual* messages are overwhelmingly important in shaping a judgement, although tone of voice is also significant. The word 'chemistry' is often used to explain why people are attracted or repulsed by a particular member of the opposite sex. We now know that we can be influenced unconsciously by sense of smell, but this has nothing to do with body odours or perfumes that we might consciously notice. We secrete substances called pheromones, which are said to unconsciously affect sexual response. However, if we don't like the look of somebody we may not get close enough to be influenced by the chemistry.

If you do get closer to someone whose visual and voice impressions are 'bad', but whose sexual chemistry is 'good', then you will begin to feel confused. Many of the classic tempestuous and tragic relationships in romantic fiction, and some in real life, result from such conflicts between how a person looks, sounds and acts, and how that person stirs the compelling chemistry of sexuality.

The Unconscious Computer

I want to emphasise that the process of forming a judgement at first sight is largely unconscious; we can't easily say how or why we respond as we do. It's as if we were linked to a super-efficient sub-conscious computer which switches on automatically whenever we meet an unknown man or woman. This computer sends us instant, instinctive messages about our like or dislike of that person.

By becoming more aware of this unconscious process, and especially through working systematically with the Dream Lover, you can enhance your ability to understand, choose and control what happens to you when you meet someone new.

The unconscious computer is impeccably logical and works as fast as light, but it has little or no common-sense! This is how it works: a large amount of visual information about the newly met person is picked up. At a glance we register impressions about his or her age, sex, size, shape, colour, facial expression, body posture and body language, clothing and other body adornments. You may not consciously note that he parts his hair on the right, or that her left hand is held clenched tightly, but your unconscious computer will. It will also pick up tiny details about quality of voice, tone, accent, vocabulary, etc.

Next, our mental computers disregard common-sense and begin to make simplistic, stereotyped comparisons, looking for the *emotional* meaning of the visual and auditory data being picked up. Unconsciously, we flash through all our past experiences of other men and women, not forgetting what we have gleaned from myth, fairy tales, the TV, magazines, books and history lessons. These memories, taken all together, make up the inner pictures of the opposite sex that we all carry.

These items from our past are already sorted into just two, mutually exclusive categories: Good and Bad. Anything about the other's appearance that reminds us of a Good experience in the past will tend to make us like the stranger. Conversely, anything that is categorised as Bad in our memory banks will leave us with a vague feeling of dislike for the person we have just met.

Now, if your computer were speaking aloud, this is a small sample of what you might hear as it goes through its lightning process:

'She wears her hair like my kid sister . . . does she expect me to look after her all the time?'

'He's wearing spectacles . . . I hope he's not too brainy.'

'Why is she talking so loudly . . . is she the bossy type?'

'He's very tall . . . oh God! I hope he's not like that lanky jerk Simon.'

I've gone into the unconscious processes that take place at a first meeting in some detail because it is this unconscious judgement that colours our initial impressions, and may well be enough to turn us off the other person before we get to the stage of making conscious, rational judgements.

By working on the Dream Lover you can build up a much fuller picture of how your unconscious content can help or hinder your relationships, especially at the initial stages. Of course, many dreams involve men and women we already know, and I will consider these in the next chapter. In this section I want to concentrate on the unknown men and women we encounter in dreams.

Blind Dates in Dreams

In many ways these dreams resemble blind dates in real life. But there is one crucial difference: the stranger in your dream is a figure that you yourself created. However you picture this stranger he or she has been dreamed up out of your own imagination. As such, these figures offer a fruitful avenue for exploration of your deeper feelings and attitudes towards the opposite sex.

The following dream, related by a forty-year-old male accountant, is a good example of such dreams:

> I'm playing the male lead in a formal, cultural play, probably
> Shakespeare. My co-star is this weird little woman. I mean *really*
> little. She is small enough to be a dwarf, dressed in Elizabethan
> costume. I feel panicky. The audience will think this is a farce. I
> watch her, anxiously waiting for her to speak her lines, and I
> realise she is becoming even smaller, shrinking before my eyes.
> As she shrinks her face falls off — it was a mask — but below
> this is another, smaller mask. This also falls off. She shrinks
> down to the size of a pin-head, shedding a succession of masks
> all the time. She gets too small to see at all. I'm left feeling
> puzzled and frightened. Although I can't see her, I know she is
> still there; what does the audience think of all this? I have to
> carry on alone somehow. I wake up in a sweat, with a great deal
> of foreboding, and I was depressed all day.

Apart from the striking central image of the shrinking woman, this dream is interesting because of the way it is presented. It is openly stated that this is a play, a drama acted out before an audience. It is surprising how often a dreamer's mind chooses a theatrical setting: 'We were making a movie . . .' or 'I was watching a film . . .' are common openings when people relate their dreams.

It's as if our unconscious was reminding us that we've been busy writing scripts again, and that the best way to find out more is to ask the author.

One of the easiest ways of doing this is to systematically question yourself about the meaning of the dream symbols, using a simple association technique. In the exercise below we can use the 'shrinking woman' dream to illustrate how each step of the process works in practice.

Association Exercise

1 First, select the items in the dream that you find most puzzling. Using our example dream, we might make a list something like this:

> Actress
> Dwarf
> Mask
> Shrinking

and so on.

2 Write the first item at the top of a sheet of paper and add the words: '. . . reminds me of.' The first item on the list is 'Actress', so you would write down the phrase: 'Actress reminds me of . . .'

3 Then, without pause and without thinking about it, repeat the phrase aloud to yourself ten times, each time writing down the *first* thing that comes into your head, no matter how silly it seems. For example, 'Actress reminds me of . . . Claire. Actress reminds me of . . . footlights. Actress reminds me of . . . gin . . . applause . . . bows . . . forgotten lines . . . school play . . . nothing . . . oh dear! . . . worry.'

4 Repeat the same sequence with each item on the list in turn. (For example, Dwarf reminds me of . . . mask, reminds me of . . . shrinking reminds me of . . ., etc.)

The key thing is speed. The technique relies on taking yourself by surprise. In effect you are prodding yourself with a rapid-fire series of questions, in the hope that the rational censor of your everyday mind will become flustered enough to blurt out some interesting truths.

Don't forget that you can treat *everything* in a dream as a separate symbol and use the association exercise on it: the weather (Fog reminds me of London); clothing (Ruffs remind me of Elizabethan . . . Elizabeth!); a turn of phrase even (You'll Pay For This reminds me of my father . . .).

You can go further still into your memories and associations by processing the words that come up in answer to the original phrase. In our example, if you look again at section three, you will see that the dreamer could follow up his curiosity about Claire, or School Plays, or Worry, by repeating the phrase, 'Claire reminds me of . . .' and so on.

The association exercise is an excellent way of warming up a dream for further work and I would recommend beginners in dream interpretation to spend some time playing with the technique. One result of such practice will be a clearer picture of your own frankness with yourself about the personal meaning of your dream images. You may be surprised at how critical or repressive you can be about your own deeper feelings and thoughts.

Once you have mastered association work though, I would recommend keeping it in reserve, as a start-up technique for dreams that don't respond to the other, less mechanistic approaches that we will be using later in the book.

John's Story

Our forty-year-old accountant (let's call him John), having gone through the association exercise on his dream is left with an expanded web of memories, trains of thought and feeling, connections with past events and people. At this stage he may be able to start to make more sense of the dream spontaneously — intuitively if you like — but if deeper insights and understanding still elude the dreamer, what next?

At this stage of your dream work I suggest you do nothing much. Don't worry at it. Simply keep the dream symbols and associations at the back of your mind for a week or so, allowing yourself to muse quietly on any particular symbol that interests you from time to time. Your aim should be to leave space in your consciousness for the dream and its meaning to develop naturally, without forcing an immediate rigid interpretation onto it.

What can you expect to happen if you allow yourself to meditate on the dream for a few days in this way? In John's case, the results of staying with the dream gave him several useful insights into his own personality and some strong clues to his problems with women.

John describes himself as a quiet type, sensible and conservative. He uncovered negative associations about theatrical people, using words like 'show-off' and 'attention seekers'. On the other hand he expressed dissatisfaction with his career, saying he would like to work more closely with people, although he couldn't see any way of doing this. I wondered whether his somewhat timid and self-effacing manner covered a deeper yearning for acknowledgement and contact.

Looking more closely at the image of the shrinking, masked woman, what was it saying about his relationship with his Dream Lover? His inner woman is stunted, and becoming smaller. Her true nature cannot be seen, for, every time she drops a mask, there is another underneath. Although he himself is playing the male lead, and occupies the centre stage, his attention is focused on *her* unwelcome theatricality. Yet when she is finally banished from sight, he is left feeling anxious and uneasy, facing the audience alone.

Over and over again in work with the Dream Lover we will see the process of attributing parts of our own personality which we dislike, neglect or deny, projected onto figures of the opposite sex. In John's case, his own unresolved dilemmas about showing off, blowing his own trumpet, being the centre of attention, etc., are neatly transferred in the dream onto the woman. It is *she* (not he) who never reveals her true nature. It is *she* (not he) who shrinks out of sight.

When I gently suggested to John that the Dream Lover reflected some of his own qualities he was initially upset. He disliked demonstrative, extravert, 'theatrical' women, so how could this have anything to do with him? He would normally feel dislike at first sight of, say, a heavily made-up woman, dramatically dressed and bejewelled, if he met such a person at a party.

The visual clues alone would convince him that he knew he and she would not get on well. He preferred the quiet type of woman, who would match his own rather shy and reserved self-image.

Yet playing it safe had not produced much satisfaction, and he had a long history of failed relationships. Which is not surprising, for by supressing the colourful side of himself and choosing safe partners who mirrored his lack of personal self-confidence, he cut himself off from the possibility of having more exciting and creative relationships with women who were more than just clones of himself.

The key factor for John in acknowledging this was the *feeling* he was left with at the end of the dream. When he had finally got rid of the Actress part of himself he was left feeling anxious, uneasy, alone and *incomplete*. After all, if the Actress really was a dangerous and alien part of himself he should have felt joy and relief when she faded away. Instead, he felt bereft.

The Shrinking Actress represented a neglected potential within John for more playfulness, colour and sociability, and pointed the way to creative changes in many areas of his life. The Dream Lover in this case, although initially puzzling and unwelcome, had presented him with the germ of an idea that would help him grow and expand out of his safe but limiting life situation.

CHAPTER 6

HAVEN'T WE MET BEFORE?

REAL PEOPLE IN DREAMS: Janet's Dream —
The 'You-and-Me' Exercise — Ruth's Dream

REAL PEOPLE IN DREAMS

The Dream Lover is a composite figure that we make up
rather like a patch-work quilt, from our own imagination
and from the impressions gathered from real-life encounters
with the opposite sex.

When we 'dream up' a stranger, it is relatively easy to
acknowledge our creation as a symbol of our relationship
with the personal inner man or woman. But what if your
dream features a real person — husband, lover, friend,
acquaintance, relative, work colleague, neighbour? Is your
dream showing you how they really are, or are you projecting onto them some part of your own personality?

There can be no categoric answer to this question. The
wisest course is to consider such dreams from both points of
view and keep an open mind. We are, after all, faced with
the same paradox in our real-life dealings with others,
especially when there is a lack of mutual understanding
between us. 'Is it me or is it her?' asks the puzzled lover,
recounting a row he's just had with his girl-friend. I for one
would hesitate to judge, except to suggest, tentatively,
'Perhaps it's a bit of both.'

One can never fully know another person. Inevitably, one

only sees part of the whole personality. We have all had the experience of hearing someone described in glowing terms by one acquaintance and heavily criticised by another. And we all know how we ourselves bring out or cover up various parts of our personality, depending on who we are with and what roles we are in.

Perhaps people are more transparent than you realise; we may unconsciously pick up much more information about each other than we think. This unconscious knowledge would then modify or enhance our view of real people when they appear in our dreams.

We may not notice subtle sexual signals in the office or supermarket, and then be surprised by erotic dreams featuring people that we've never consciously thought of in that way. Or, we may dream of an intimate partner, but in an unfamiliar setting, acting in some strange and uncharacteristic way: 'Never in my wildest dreams would I have imagined him acting like that!'

On the other hand, such dreams could be reflecting our *own* unacknowledged fantasy hopes and fears, in which case the 'real' dream figure may have little to do with the other person's reality, and a lot to do with hidden parts of our own personality.

This is why I believe that no one can tell you categorically which is the right way to view real people in your dreams. As always, only the dreamer can finally decide which alternative is more correct.

What concerns us in this book is how to discover new insights into the ways we think and feel about the opposite sex, and to learn more about the ways we think and feel about ourselves in the light of that relationship. As a general rule, therefore, I recommend that you regard a real-life figure in your dreams primarily as a *symbol* of the opposite sex for you. You can then start to consider what it is in your own life that this particular person has been chosen to symbolise. The figure may represent something of yourself that you love but can only find in the opposite sex, or something of yourself that you dislike, and disown, projecting this quality onto the opposite sex.

Janet's Dream

Many dreams concern the Dream Lover in the guise of the current partner in an unusual setting, and by looking closer at the roles we fall into on these occasions, we see more clearly how a partner can collude with and reinforce our somewhat rigid definitions of what a Man is, and what a Woman is.

The following dream, related by Janet, a woman in her thirties, is typical of such dreams:

> I was wading through the sea towards a red-and-white striped refreshment booth, which floated in the sun-lit water about 100 metres from the shore. Paul, (her husband), was leading the way and I was finding it difficult to keep up with him. For one thing, I was distracted by the fish in the water. They looked so beautiful. I tried to catch one, but they were too quick and slippery.
>
> Finally, Paul stopped, and, putting his arm into the water, caught a fish and held it up, as if it were the easiest thing in the world. He held it out for me to take, but it wriggled and slipped from my hands immediately. He caught another, and the same thing happened; I couldn't hold on to it and I felt really foolish and useless.

The 'You-and-Me' Exercise

This is a two-step exercise. First, you attempt to obtain a simple clear picture of the other person in the dream, in this case Paul. I asked Janet to give me five key words that described Paul's essential character.

'He's very *practical*,' she said, and went on: 'He's so *calm* . . . He gets things done without a fuss . . . He's good at *planning ahead*, it's usually him that works out what we are to do and how to do it. He doesn't wait for things to happen, he takes the *initiative*. And I think he's *strong*, he has an inner strength that I find very reassuring.'

With these few phrases Janet had sketched some of the fundamental masculine virtues that she (and many other women I'm sure) expects in her ideal man: and she was very happy to be living with such a man.

In dreamwork, however, we want to look a little deeper than this, so I would like to draw attention to the fact that, by painting this picture of the positive male virtues, she was at the same time painting out these same virtues for herself. In her dream this situation is reflected by the Dream Lover/ Paul. *He* leads the way, *he* takes the initiative and competently catches the fish; she is left feeling foolish, and useless in the practical aspects of life.

The point I want to make is this: it is not because the Dream Lover/Paul is a *man* that he has practical skills, calmness, inner strength, etc., and it is not because she is a *woman* that Janet finds herself helpless in handling the practical side of life. It is rather because each person in this partnership has chosen to develop a different part of the whole personality. Janet could, if she wished to, decide to start developing those parts of her own potential that at the moment are held for her by the Dream Lover in her dreams, and by Paul in her waking life.

Starting such changes is not easy, as you will discover when you turn to the second part of the 'You-and-Me' exercise. To do this, simply take the five-word sketch of the other person and repeat the words aloud as if they were statements about yourself.

So here we have Janet saying:

'I am very practical.'
'I am calm.'
'I am good at planning.'
'I take the initiative.'
'I have an inner strength that I find very reassuring.'

She found it difficult to speak the words aloud. She blushed, stammered, protested and laughed at herself. Describing Paul in this way made her feel good on the whole.

53

But describing herself in a similar vein made her squirm with embarrassment.

Why is it that this simple exercise can be so hard to perform? I believe it is difficult because it often directly contradicts our cosy certainties about what men and women are. Furthermore, I'd say that the degree to which you find this part of the exercise ridiculous or embarrassing will give you a clue to the strength of your resistance to change from your habitual gender images and assumptions.

By some strange, masochistic quirk of human nature, we often find it is just as difficult to claim and develop positive qualities for ourselves as it is to own up to our more negative qualities. Janet discovered how uncomfortable she felt when she tried to lay even a verbal claim on the virtues which she saw as belonging strictly to her husband's male territory.

Ruth's Dream

The following dream raises further interesting possibilities for self-exploration because the Dream Lover appears simultaneously in two contradictory guises: the Good man and the Bad man. The dreamer is a woman in her late twenties, and I shall call her Ruth. Oliver is her lover, and Jack is her older brother:

> Oliver and I were racing hand-in-hand up a wonderful spiral
> staircase. We were virtually flying up the steps in great
> bounding leaps. I felt exhilarated by the speed as we circled
> higher and higher. Then, suddenly, I turned a corner and fell
> over Jack, who was lying as if dead, across the stairway. He was
> such a heavy lump. He wasn't dead, just unconscious or asleep,
> and he completely blocked the way. Oliver had disappeared,
> and I just sat down feeling flat and depressed. I couldn't go any
> further.

When Ruth did the first stage of the 'You-and-Me' exercise, she chose a set of five key statements to describe Oliver, and another five to describe Jack. The two lists were:

Oliver is:
  Exciting
  Free
  Spiritual
  Adventurous
  Self-centred

Jack is:
  Boring, a drag
  Irritating
  Selfish
  Unaware of others
  Clever in a stupid kind of way

Apart from both men being selfish or self-centred, they seem to have nothing in common. Oliver seems to have mostly good qualities and Jack embodies several of the classic bad aspects of 'men as a whole'.

We all seem to spend a lot of time classifying members of the opposite sex into good and bad, and once we've applied the label it's quite difficult to remove or amend it. It seems we feel uncomfortable until we've decided whether a particular man or woman is 'nice' or 'nasty', because ambivalence makes us anxious and uncertain about the right response.

For Ruth, then, the second stage of the exercise took her straight to the heart of the difficulties which arise from our tendency to polarise human qualities into good and bad and/or male and female. The central dilemma is this: once we have separated human qualities into good and bad, we become anxious and defensive if the two show any signs of coming together again. It confuses us because it threatens a neatly labelled, cut-and-dried self-identity.

The second step of the exercise is designed to do just that: it will create an initially confusing, 'coming together' sensation, because the opposites *are* coming together, within the identity of the dreamer.

So long as Ruth regards the dream as a simple observation

of two different types of men, she remains in the role of a mere spectator. The conflict and contrast between Oliver and Jack can seem to have nothing much to do with Ruth. However, when she came to apply the descriptions of both men to herself, she was very confused and declared the whole exercise nonsensical.

'I can't be exciting, adventurous *and* boring, can I?'

'Why not?'

'Because if you are one thing, you can't be another.'

'Perhaps a person can be *sometimes* exciting and *sometimes* boring?'

In this exchange with Ruth, I was challenging her fixed, either/or view of herself and others: either people are one thing or they *must* be the opposite. Of herself, Ruth was saying, 'If I'm not adventurous, I am boring . . . if I am not irritable, I will be spiritual . . . if I am free, I will not be selfish.' The truth I am sure is that she is actually a bit of both, in each case.

This dilemma of self-identity, the feeling of having to be one thing or another, has its roots in the universal childhood problem of how to be a 'good' child in the eyes of one's family and how to avoid being 'bad'. This makes Ruth's choice of 'bad brother Jack', as the symbolic obstacle to her upward progress in the dream, of special importance.

In reality her brother was identified as the black sheep by the whole family, with a reputation for being sulky, irritating and selfish, although he was also clearly clever and intelligent. In contrast, Ruth carried the family role of 'good girl' — willing, compliant, avoiding conflicts at home, and doing well at university. However, since completing her degree, she had less and less contact with her family, moving away to a town at the other end of the country.

It is not appropriate here to present a complete case history of Ruth's problems in relating to her family, but the following brief notes will give some idea of the important forgotten issues that can re-emerge when we record and work on an average-seeming dream.

Ruth's initial focus is on Jack, the unconscious and depressing symbol of the family, which blocks her development, but on reflection she soon realises that her feeling that he is boring, irritating and unaware applies equally to her parents. Father, who is only interested in material success and security, and mother, who has no life of her own: 'She's only interested in when I'm going to find a good husband, settle down, and raise a family.' Both parents are somewhat dominating in their insistence that they always know best, with little acknowledgement that their children may have equally valid ideas on how to conduct their lives, even though the children are now adults in their own right.

This on-going conflict between our needs for self-assertion, and feelings of disloyalty and guilt towards parents is not to be underestimated. You will begin to realise how difficult it can be to clearly separate yourself from 'them' when you come to consider family influences in Chapter 13. The struggle to establish a separate identity and gender role, apart from the models offered by parents and others, becomes internalised, and can last well into adult life.

Jack allows his resistance and resentment to his parents to show, but in a passive and self-defeating way. He has not yet found the courage to stand up for himself and take the risks and responsibilities of following his own ideas. Ruth's antagonism, and reservations about her parents' scale of values, is more hidden, yet she also senses the need to distance herself from them in order to work out her own values and life-style.

Part of the difficulty for Ruth is that there is more than a grain of truth in her parents' conventional attitudes. It is self-evident that a measure of financial security and stability is important to a sense of well-being, but there is much more to life than material comfort and safe predictability. We all need to work out a compromise between the opposing attractions of freedom and security, adventure and routine, risk and boredom — a compromise that satisfies our own true natures.

Until Ruth comes to terms with her inner uncertainty, and strikes her own balance between security and adventure, she is likely to bring these issues into her adult relationships, creating much misunderstanding, confusion and dissatisfaction. Perhaps she will allow a partner like Oliver to lead her a merry dance, but ultimately she may resent his irresponsibility. She may then rebound into a relationship with a more sensible man, reliable but somewhat dull, and then resent him for boring her. In any event, she will eventually have to decide where *she* stands, and take responsibility for finding a partner whose values more closely match her own.

CHAPTER 7

GETTING TO KNOW YOU

GIVING THE DREAM LOVER A VOICE: Dream Dialogues
— The Method

GIVING THE DREAM LOVER
A VOICE

The vital ingredient in all successful relationships is communication. Each stage of the relationship poses its own
problems and challenges, but if either partner is unwilling
or unable to communicate adequately there is little chance of
progressing past the initial encounter and attraction.

One of the commonest complaints made about partners
and spouses is, 'He (or she) won't talk about it.' And
whenever one partner breaks the vital link of communication, the other partner will feel distress, sometimes to the
point of desperation, for, when real communication is with-
held, we are forced to fall back on speculation: 'What's
wrong with him? What's wrong with me? What did I say or
do that she doesn't like? What the hell does he want? I
wonder what she really thinks? I wonder how I can cheer
him up?' and so on.

We all know how hurtful and worrying it can be when
someone we are involved with goes 'off the air' for no
obvious reason. And the hurt *may* be intentional. The silent
sulk is a commonly used weapon in all sorts of relationships, designed to punish and control the other person. The

wooden face, the colourless voice, the indifference and withdrawal are intended to create anxiety and guilt in our partners, and to increase our own feelings of power and importance. If we were to state our grievances, demands or criticisms openly, we would lose this power, or rather we would be letting go of a destructive, infantile ploy, and dealing with our partners on an equal adult footing.

More often though we withdraw behind our wall of silence for defensive rather than offensive reasons, especially during the early 'getting to know you' phase of a relationship.

We all have a negative side to our self-image. There will be parts of the personality or personal history that we have decided to keep quiet about, and we will be reluctant to share these feelings of inadequacy or failure: until, that is, we have got to know the other person well enough to trust our more vulnerable side to scrutiny, and possible rejection. Hence, the awkward silences and embarrassments that crop up as we are becoming better acquainted.

With care, trust and sensitive communication, we can create a relationship that is safe enough for us to start letting go of our defensive habits, but without good communication the relationship may falter and die during these preliminary stages.

Dream Dialogues

Communication is just as vital in work with the Dream Lover as it is in real life, but, fortunately, whatever our mistakes and however clumsy our attempts at understanding, we will never irreparably harm our relationship with the inner man or woman. The Dream Lover is truly a partner for life.

So far, we have learned to use simple techniques to question ourselves about the Dream Lover: the association exercise gives valuable clues to the significance of strangers in dreams, and the You-and-Me exercise helps us see how we tend to allow our partners and other people to carry parts of our own potential for us, while we disown these qualities in ourselves.

Now I want to introduce another method of working with the Dream Lover, one that will enable you to question your dream men and women directly. I have borrowed this technique, which I call Dream Dialogue, from gestalt psychology.

This exercise is best done in private, because it may involve talking aloud to yourself! But don't worry. In this context, talking to yourself doesn't mean you are going crazy. It simply indicates your ability to re-enter a child-like state, where toys, animals and other things have their own imagined voices. As a child, you used this ability for creative play and development. Now, as an adult, you can redevelop this skill and use it to gain personal insights into the meaning of your Dream Lover.

The Method

1 Select a dream figure of the opposite sex that particularly interests or puzzles you, and give it a name, for example, 'The Limping Man', or 'Miss Blue Shoes'. If the figure is someone you know, invent a new, more descriptive name, and use that instead of the person's real name. To take an example from the previous chapter, Janet's husband could be renamed 'The Fisherman' or 'Mr Practical'.

2 Take a sheet of paper and write down a list of questions that you would like the Dream Lover to answer. Typical questions would be: Where do you come from? What do you want? What can you teach me? Why have you come into my dreams now? What do you need now? What is your real name? What is your gift to me?, etc.

3 Take the first question on the list and repeat it to yourself, either mentally or aloud.

4 Form a mental picture of the person you are questioning, and imagine the reply. *Quickly* write down the first answer that occurs to you, regardless of how silly, irrelevant or comical it may seem.

The answer can come in the form of a single word, or a riddle, or a perfectly ordinary conversational reply. The response may be an inarticulate sound, a shout, a giggle, a sob — or even simply a gesture. Whatever your impulse is, just write it down, without pausing to think it over.

5 Go straight on to the next question on your list. Alternatively, a new question may arise out of the previous reply, or indeed, out of the *lack* of reply. If, for instance, you ask, 'Where do you come from?', and there is no apparent answer, you could then ask, 'Why is it a secret?' or 'What prevents you talking to me?'

6 Continue with your series of questions and answers until you are satisfied with the result for now. Some of these dialogues flow fluently and easily, and you may find yourself rapidly covering several sheets of paper. At other times the dialogue is finished and you have the information you seek, after one or two key questions.

7 When you are a little more familiar with this technique, you may want to dispense with the paper-work and conduct the exercise with a tape recorder. If you use this method you will be able to listen out for changes in the tone of your voice when you record the answers. If you find yourself putting on a special voice — wheedling, angry or sad — for the Dream Lover, this will give you additional insight into his or her meaning for you.

Note Apart from direct questions to the Dream Lover figure, dream dialogue can be used to understand other significant objects in the dream. Taking Janet's dream again as an example, she might want to go deeper into the meaning of the elusive fish, by asking a series of questions and imagining the replies: 'What are you? How can I hold on to you? What part of me do you represent? What use are you to me?' and so on.

The fact that you alone have to provide both sides of the dialogue is obvious, and perhaps this will make you sceptical of the results. So may I remind you again of the central idea behind this work: when you talk to your Dream Lover, you are actually relating to a part of yourself. The male or female figure is your own creation, which you have brought into the dream because it has a relevant message of significance to you at this time.

Like all the exercises in this book, dream dialogue is simple to describe and understand. But its effectiveness and skilful use depends on your willingness to overcome self-consciousness and scepticism. Try it out, and give yourself enough time and practice to develop your skill in the way that suits you best.

CHAPTER 8
SWEET DREAMS

SEXUAL ENCOUNTERS WITH THE DREAM LOVER

Sooner or later, the initial exploratory phase in a relationship will lead to a point of choice, between remaining just good friends, or taking the 'getting to know you' process a crucial stage further — into the bedroom.

Sexuality is a major preoccupation: in our culture, especially in recent decades, sex has been the focus of passionate, widespread and seemingly endless debate. Vast amounts of information and advice are currently available on how to do it, and what you should think and feel about doing it. An army of experts, researchers and commentators constantly updates our knowledge of the techniques, morals, politics, fashions, dangers, and socio-economic implications of sex.

Clearly there is no shortage of external advice and guidance on sexuality. Yet despite this broad and open debate within our contemporary society, many people still find themselves bedevilled by unexpected complexities, confusions and conflicts in their sex lives.

Why is it that the sexual aspect of a relationship can be so confusing? I believe that the root of the problem is that sexual activity simply *cannot* be separated out and considered in isolation from the rest of life. In reality, a great many other relationship issues are inseparably woven into this apparently simple straightforward gratification of a primary human instinct.

Inevitably, we bring to our physical love-making a more or less hidden, and seldom discussed, collection of *extra* hopes, fears and expectations — a 'hidden agenda' that represents our ideas of what sex means in terms of emotional and psychological fulfilment. Problems are bound to arise when there is a significant mismatch between the hidden agendas brought together by the couple concerned.

It is easy to delude ourselves that we know what sex means to us, and that our partner will, in some mysterious instinctive or intuitive way, know and agree with our assumptions, without our having to say a word about our private psychological landscape. Quite commonly, a couple will spend years together with only the woolliest notion of what their partner expects, and with an equally vague awareness of what they themselves are looking for, beyond the physical act of sex. And yet our sexual partner is often the last person that we would talk to about the *additional* needs and expectations which we feel are enshrined in the sex act.

So I invite you now to consider this question: 'What does sex really mean for me — what does sex symbolise?'

Reasons for Sex

Your list of reasons for sex may range from ill-defined romantic aspirations, ('our two souls merge and become one'), to explicit, practical goals ('I want to have a baby'). Whatever the nature of your hopes and fears, this list will form the basis for the hidden agenda against which you judge the fulfilment or failure of your sex life, regardless of how good in bed you are together.

Here is a small sample of the ways in which people have told me what they want in sex:

It brings us closer together.

It creates good feelings.

I feel cared for.

I want/we want children.

I can communicate feelings of affection and love.

It confirms I am a real woman (or a real man).

It brings emotional release. (Feelings are often held in check through physical tension in the body. The act of sex can relax us enough for the feelings to emerge and we find ourselves laughing or crying 'for no reason'.)

I am proud of my body.

I enjoy the erotic fantasies and images more than the physical sex.

It helps me to forget myself; it gets me out of myself. (Sex can temporarily abolish feelings of loneliness and separation.)

I am doing him/her a favour . . . he/she is much more interested in sex than I am . . . men/women always are.

Sex is what's expected of a wife/husband. (That is to say that sex is a duty.)

It binds us together.

Sex is over-rated. I can't see the point. There are many more important things in life.

It's healthy; it keeps me healthy. (And young?)

Sex means I'm still attractive. (And lovable? And powerful?)

I feel he/she must still like me, because we still sleep together, despite the rows. (Deeper issues of self-worth and self-esteem are often linked with sexual acceptability.)

I deserve good sex after a hard day at the office. (Sex can be seen as a reward for being good.)

The list is seemingly endless. Perhaps we are capable of attaching any or all of our wider human aspirations and emotional needs onto a sexual relationship?

Do you see your own half-hidden expectations reflected in any of these statements? Clearly, sex can mean many things to different people, and knowing our own agendas is the essential first step in improving this aspect of our relationships.

This is why sexual encounters with the Dream Lover can be of unique value in helping us to explore deeper feelings and attitudes towards sexuality. What goes on in the dream bedroom is an authentic and often explicit summary of our personal sexual situations.

Defining a Sexual Dream

Before you start on this aspect of your dreamwork, you may like to ask yourself, 'What is a sexual dream?'

This may seem a redundant question but many dreams which do not even include a human sexual object *could* be interpreted as symbolically sexual if we decide to take on the assumptions of Freudian psychology.

Most people in our culture are familiar with the cliché symbols of sexuality that have arisen from this source: the snake is the penis, the cave is the vagina, and so on. You may decide to look at your dreams in this way, and indeed there is much to be discovered from exploring the universal symbolism of male and female archetypes.

However, for the early stages of dreamwork I would recommend that you confine your attention to dreams in which you feel sexual excitement, and in which the images are obviously sexual. Then there will be no doubt in your mind that the dreams you choose to help you explore your sexuality are indeed about sex for you. Otherwise you may get confused by a situation in which every dream of a train entering a tunnel or of a bucket being lowered into a well *could* be about sex.

(*Note*: unfortunately, feelings other than pleasure and excitement — such as fear and rage — can also become strongly associated with sex. This problem, which is often a root cause of nightmare dreams, is discussed in Chapter 10.)

Here then is a selection of excerpts from dreams where the sexual content is obvious and explicit:

1 (Male dreamer) . . . I enter a shabby, barely furnished bedroom. A man and a woman are making love on the bed. They are both grey, with loose, bloodless skin, looking half-dead, with no vitality. They are making love mechanically, with no life, no enjoyment . . .

2 (Female dreamer) . . . he (an ex-lover) and I are sharing a bath together. At first I try to keep to my own end, but there's not enough room, and so we come together and start to make love. I'm excited by the warm water and the closeness of his body. Suddenly, there's a knock on the door . . . it's my mother outside the bathroom. She wants to come in, and is saying, 'Why have you locked the door . . . what are you up to in there?' I feel awful, terribly guilty and in a panic . . .

3 (Male dreamer) . . . a Persian king and his entourage have come to rebuild the factory where I work (although in real life I work in an office). He says that we must make extensive alterations and pay attention to the quality of the decor. He pulls off a strip of wall-paper. Underneath it, there are lions' faces embossed in the plaster that were hidden behind the paper. Whilst he is busy, a beautiful young oriental woman comes and stands beside me and begins to act very seductively, taking me by the hand and leading me towards a couch in the corner. I feel very aroused and pleased that she likes me, but also very embarrassed; I'm not sure whether she belongs to the king, or whether she is free and available to me. Meanwhile, I am anxious that he shouldn't see us together . . .

4 (Female dreamer) . . . I am lying naked and face down over a vaulting horse in a gymnasium. My husband is going to make love to me from behind, but he is using a felt-tip pen! (In the dream it was exciting and pleasurable, but now I'm really puzzled by the pen . . . what does that mean?) . . .

Themes of guilt, exposure, frustration and interruption are common in sexual dreams, and you will not need to be a psychotherapist to spot this in dreams 2 and 3. Indeed, the woman dreamer in the second example only needed to remember and record the dream to be able to focus on her mother's own sexual anxiety and guilt, and the various ways in which these tensions were transferred to her as a child. It is sometimes easy to see the origins of underlying feelings about sex, and I believe that our hidden agendas are largely written by our parents and other prominent figures in the family during our formative years, and especially during puberty.

In the fourth example, the central puzzling item is the felt-tip pen, and the dreamer's main question is, 'What does this mean?' This dream, therefore, would be a good choice for the association technique described in Chapter 5 (see p. 45). Using this technique would rapidly help her to assemble further information about what a pen means for her (for example, 'felt-tipped pens remind me of . . . felt-tipped pens are used for . . .' and so on).

In doing so, she would also be getting in touch with her unconscious picture of what her husband's sexuality really offers her, and more broadly, perhaps, what sex implies for her in general: why should a man make love to her with a pen and not a penis, and why in a gymnasium?

Another technique we have already used, Dream Dialogue (see p. 60), could usefully be applied to the mother outside the bathroom door in dream 2, or to the Persian king in dream 3. This might well bring out into the open much unfinished business with parents, dating from adolescence and earlier, thus providing an opportunity to come to terms in an adult way with long-buried fears and resentments about parental strictures on sex.

Apart from reminding you here that all the dreamwork techniques can be applied to any kind of dream as soon as you learn them, I'd like also to introduce a fresh way of working with your Dream Lover material. The technique is again simple, in fact you undoubtedly used it frequently as a child. But as an adult you may have largely forgotten it, or if you do happen to catch yourself doing it, you feel a bit guilty and snap out of it as quickly as possible. I am referring to daydreaming.

This activity is aptly named, for the physical and mental

state of the daydreamer closely resembles a sleeping dreamer. The body is relaxed, the eyes are half-closed, the facial expression is abstracted, the breathing is often intermittent and shallow; we can tell at a glance that such a person is 'miles away'.

You will know from experience how deeply absorbing a daydream can be, how pictures and dialogue seem to arise unbidden before your inner eye and ear. Although some may say that we are wasting time indulging in escapist fantasies, I would like to propose a different point of view. Used in the right place and at the right time, an inborn capacity for daydreaming offers us a fruitful new way of consciously and deliberately re-entering and exploring our dreams.

Deliberate Daydreaming

The only problem you are likely to have in using this technique is in overcoming the psychological blocks that will have almost certainly been set up in your childhood. Just consider for a moment how strongly schoolchildren are discouraged from daydreaming in the classroom, and how this 'non-productive' activity is generally frowned upon by adults.

So if you want to use daydreaming for your dreamwork, start by giving yourself permission! Your purpose is to create a state of mind where you can easily re-enter the dream situation that you have chosen to work on.

To do this, find a time and place that is quiet and free from the possibility of interruptions. Make yourself comfortable (if you lie down, though, you are likely to drift off into true sleep whilst daydreaming).

Go through a bodily relaxation routine, focusing on each part of your body in turn from your feet to your face, and letting them become looser and heavier. Tell yourself you are deeply relaxed, and allow your breathing to become fuller and deeper.

70

With your eyes closed, re-run the dream that you are working on, letting your imagination work to the full. Try to re-live it with all your inner senses — how it looked, how it felt, how it sounded, even how it smelt and tasted — as vividly and convincingly as possible. Some people prefer to imagine themselves in a darkened cinema, with the dream being replayed on a screen before their eyes.

Now, what you are looking for is the continuation of the dream, the next few scenes which might have come after the end of the actual dream. You want to know what would have happened next, where it would have led, if you hadn't woken up at that point. To facilitate this, you need *not try*; I know this sounds paradoxical but the more you try to force these things the more elusive they become. So just relax into a musing speculative mood, and enjoy watching what happens in your imagination, with your judgement suspended for a while.

Richard's Dream

I have reserved discussion of the first dream in the series of examples given above until now, because I want to use it to illustrate how the daydreaming technique can work in practice.

Richard, the dreamer in this example, recalls a childhood marred by the unsettling and destructive relationship between his parents. He was particularly upset by the wildly immature displays of anger, frustration and depression indulged in by his father.

As an adult, Richard still finds himself anxious to keep a tight rein on the free expression of his feelings. He speaks and moves slowly and deliberately, and becomes tense and verbose when his self-control seems threatened by emotional upsets. He describes sex with his wife as if it were an obligation, a rather unfeeling chore; he cannot seem to get over his fear of bringing strong feelings into an intimate relationship.

Richard's unhappiness represents a common dilemma in relationships. He both longs for and fears deep emotional contact with another, yet he feels that the only safe way to be close is to bottle-up and deny those feelings which he considers dangerous — anger, fear and grief. Unfortunately, our efforts to edit and suppress some feelings usually lead to the suppression of all feelings.

No wonder then, that his dream of love-making takes place in a monochrome bedroom, and that the couple are grey, bloodless and half-dead. Without feelings, life loses its vibrancy, colour, music and poetry. It loses its essential flavour.

When Richard used the daydreaming technique to look again at this scene, he quickly grew dissatisfied with the drab, colourless atmosphere, and began imagining colour and light flooding into the walls and the furnishings. He imagined the lovers brightening up, smiling, relaxing, and beginning to embrace without fear. This made him feel deeply moved, and he began to talk of his longing for wholeness, completion and reconciliation with his 'other half', symbolised here by the woman.

Generally, if we take dreams a stage further by using the daydreaming technique, we can expect movement in ourselves. It helps to free closed situations by encouraging the dreamer to explore further and come up with creative new solutions to the dilemmas of life. In effect, with this technique, you are asking yourself. 'What next; now what? What could be the next step?'

In Richard's case, after he had imagined the lovers' embrace, I asked him, 'What next? What do they do next?'

'They begin to talk,' he said.

'What about?'

'How they feel. They're beginning to tell each other how they feel . . . I imagine them *forgiving* each other for bad feelings in the past . . . and *I* begin to feel compassion for my poor, stupid parents.'

This, then, is the way that Richard found to move. His

existing 'hidden agenda' could be stated as, 'Sexual intimacy is dangerous, for we mustn't say how we feel, otherwise we shall be trapped in destructive conflict like my parents.'

Now he has some inkling of what he must do to change this. He must 'colour-in' his life, as he coloured-in the dream, by including his emotional side, and he must bring colour into his relationships by revealing and sharing his feelings more freely.

CHAPTER 9
'BEAUTY . . .

IDEALISATIONS OF THE OPPOSITE SEX: The Reality Gap — Princes and Frogs — The Ideal Dream Lover — The Acting Out Technique — Growing Pains — Keeping It in Perspective

IDEALISATIONS OF THE OPPOSITE SEX

The 'honeymoon stage' of a relationship is generally an exciting and happy time. Within the magic circle of our romance everything seems to be working out fine. The first flush of greater intimacy, as we play and share and joke together, rapidly builds into a conviction that nothing could possibly go wrong this time.

An important part of this conviction is our tendency to idealise the person that we are having such a good time with. Love makes us not so much blind, as partially sighted. Whereas we normally accept that people are a mixture of black and white with many shades of grey in between, during the honeymoon phase we may be incapable of seeing anything but spotless pure perfection.

We are liable to describe our lovers in the most extravagant and absolute terms. He or she is: beautiful, exciting, faultless, strong, loving, considerate, witty, creative, stylish. Our friends, steeped in the cynicism of those not in love, do best to keep their mouths shut and nod wisely at this stage.

It's important to realise that we are all, in truth, quite capable of demonstrating any or all of these wonderful qualities at any time, and especially on honeymoon. But just imagine for a moment what life would be like if one or both partners *insisted* on nothing less than perfection, *forever*. Imagine the tension: who is going to crack first? Who will be first to admit to grumpiness, selfishness, dullness or conceit?

Over-insistence on permanent perfection can trap us into a limiting and uneasy relationship, wherein we cannot relax and be our fuller, realer selves, with all our human faults and foibles, for fear of shattering the shining images of the honeymoon. And indeed, a period of critical reassessment normally takes place after the honeymoon, as the partners reassert their rights to be rather less than perfect all the time.

Some people, however, find it difficult to establish a realistic balance between honeymoon euphoria and the disillusions of the post-honeymoon phase. The uncomfortable gap between ideal and reality can then form the basis for longer-term problems that interfere with, and in extreme cases totally prevent, intimate relationships.

It is all a matter of degree. At one end of this scale is the rather romantic person who tends to view the opposite sex through (slightly) rose-tinted spectacles. At the other extreme are those who cannot tolerate any real intimacy with ordinary people, preferring instead to spend their lives in a fruitless quest for an illusory Perfect Partner.

In the latter case, the fantasy ideal has become a psychological defence, a refuge that is used to avoid the pain of coping with life's reality. The starry-eyed seeker, intent on finding Prince Charming or the Sleeping Beauty, may in fact be inwardly consumed by bitterness and grief. Characteristically, the true emotional situation is revealed by their habitual biting criticisms of the 'second-best' real people that they have dealings with. Alternatively, this profound rejection of anyone less than perfect is turned inwards, and the sufferer becomes highly self-critical, expressing constant dissatisfaction with his or her own reality and worth.

I want to discuss some of these more exaggerated patterns in greater detail here, because the idealisation syndrome does affect us all to some degree, and it is worthwhile exploring the extent to which we personally resort to this device in our relationships. In doing so, I do not suggest that everyone who indulges in wishful fantasies and romantic notions is a neurotic escapist who cannot cope with reality!

The Reality Gap

There are many ways in which an uncomfortable gap can be set up between what we expect or wish for, and our actual experience.

Sometimes, the gap is created by heavy-handed and insensitive parents or teachers, who, in trying to impart their own standards of achievement and quality, succeed only in undermining the child's self-confidence. The unfortunate child may find itself disparagingly compared with various models of perfection — a more talented or attractive brother or sister perhaps, or some more distant relative of legendary virtue.

The disturbing message that is implanted in the child is that perfection belongs to others, and is forever beyond its own reach: 'You are not good enough, but you must always strive to be.' The double-bind can be intolerable. Our natural resentment at this attack on our self-esteem cannot be expressed, for if we show anger it merely confirms that we *are* imperfect. So maybe we start to hide our true feelings, and nurse secret thoughts of revenge upon those model people we are supposed to admire. As adults, we may unconsciously impose the same double-bind on our partners, with conflicting urges to put them onto a pedestal and simultaneously cut them down to our own size.

Fantasies of ideal men or women may also be created in

76

childhood as a kind of compensation by those unfortunate enough to have lost their opposite sex parent through death or permanent separation. It is as if the painful and mysterious void left by the missing parent has to be filled somehow, and so the child begins to develop wish-fulfilling idealisations of a perfectly loving mother or father.

These may form the unconscious basis, in later life, of the restless quest for the Perfect Partner mentioned above.

Somewhat similar unconscious fantasies of perfect, loving parents may evolve in a child that needs to defend itself psychologically from the destructive reality of a cruel or indifferent opposite sex parent. Again, this early pattern may be played out far into adulthood, in the form of a hopeless search for a partner loving enough or caring enough to replace the inner fantasy.

The fact that these forms of idealisation have their beginnings in early life accounts for the power they have in influencing our adult relationships; they are powerful because they remain unconscious. As adults, we can explore and reconstruct the psychological bases for our feelings, attitudes and behaviour, and consciously modify them to some extent. But a child responds to emotional stress by automatically adapting. She does not sit down and work out a fantasy ideal deliberately; she does not think, 'I have no father, therefore I will comfort myself by creating an ideal inner image of a perfect, loving, available father.'

Princes and Frogs

Whatever its source, the myth of the Perfect Partner can create much unhappiness in our adult relationships. Unless we work to become aware of the size and strength of our own idealisations we may waste much of our life in fairy-tale quests for the Prince. Unfortunately, this futile quest sets us up to experience great disappointment, disillusion and bitterness, as each new prospective Prince turns out to be a Frog after all.

We can come to believe that it is safer to cherish our fantasies in isolation, rather than to learn to cope with the awkward reality of other people. If the gap between our idea of the Perfect Partner and the men and women we actually meet becomes too great, we might defensively choose to avoid close relationships altogether. Thus we might feel increasingly inclined to 'keep our distance', to 'worship from afar', rather than risk further disappointments.

Such isolation can lead into a deepening spiral of self-criticism, as the disappointment is turned against oneself. We can witness this process in others, and sometimes in ourselves, as we justify our loneliness by claiming some form of personal inferiority or inadequacy: 'He'd never look at *me* . . . She's way out of *my* class . . . I'd never interest a man like that . . . I can offer her nothing . . .' etc.

This problem is often complicated by a tendency to think in absolute and fixed terms. People are either one thing or another. There is no middle ground for the rich variety and change which characterise growth and the vibrancy of life in a person. If he is a Prince, everyone else, including me, must be a Frog. If he is not the Prince, he must be a Frog.

If we hope to change this situation, we must be willing to consider broader, more variegated images of ourselves and others. We are never 'finished products', with clear-cut identities and lists of qualities that are fixed and final. It is at the frayed edges of our personalities, the troubling areas of uncertainty, that we grow and develop. Whenever we become fixed and rigid, we stop growth, we limit our own life process, and we limit the scope of our relationships.

Another factor which makes it difficult to come to terms with our idealisations is the habit of seeking to realise our ideals in others rather than in ourselves.

We make the fundamental error of asking the wrong question: 'How can I find the Prince?' rather than asking: 'How can I become more Princely?'

The Ideal Dream Lover

Working with the Dream Lover, therefore, offers us a new way of confronting this impasse. Because we understand that the Dream Lover, in *all* its forms, comes from ourselves into our dreams, we can consider it as an authentic symbol of part of ourselves. Whenever we dream of a man or woman with qualities that we admire, we have an opportunity to explore and develop more of these qualities in ourselves.

How can you set about selecting the most appropriate dreams for this stage of your dreamwork? Look for examples of opposite sex figures that arouse feelings of respect, awe, admiration, envy — people who have something 'good' about them, people with skills, talents, personal qualities of character that you wish *you* could possess.

It is not uncommon for the idealised Dream Lover to appear in the form of a religious or spiritual figure — a saint, a guru, a wise man or priestess. Sometimes it will be a beautiful youth or maiden, idealising the qualities of vigour, freshness, innocence and adventure. Figures of healers, doctors and other people of benevolent authority could be included, along with artists, writers, sportsmen or others demonstrating abilities that you desire and envy.

For example, in the following dream a man in his forties sees his long-forgotten creative potential idealised in the form of an 'old flame' who has become a sculptress:

> . . . I am looking at some enormous faces carved into the rocky sides of a canyon. I have the ability to move up and down the cliff, so that I can examine details of the carving in close-up, or I can stand back and admire the overall effect. I have a feeling of pleased, almost joyous excitement. The colours and textures of the rocks are so vibrant. It is all so perfect. To think that it's possible to create such a wonderful thing!

> Then, suddenly, I'm with the artist who did this work. She reminds me very much of a girl I was in love with when I was twenty — Helen — but it's not exactly the same person. Her face seems to float about and change.

> What strikes me in the dream is her *practicality*. She's telling
> me, in a matter of fact way, the technical details of how she
> creates her sculptures, the use of dynamite to develop the rough
> shape, the finishing work and details done with power tools.
> She seems very powerful and self-assured. I feel shy and
> awkward; underneath my admiration is a strong feeling of
> sexual attraction towards her . . .

The artistic talent which had lain dormant in this man for
25 years happened to be a long-buried ambition to be a
writer. As a teenager, he had been too easily discouraged
from this desire, and had concluded that he was simply not
the artistic type. Now Helen, in her matter of fact way, is
pointing out how he could rekindle this urge by taking
practical steps to learn the *craft* of writing, rather than
bemoaning his lack of artistic temperament.

Notice how this issue is mixed up and obscured by his
sexual feelings for Helen. It is almost as if he hopes that by
possessing his idealisation sexually he can find a magical
short-cut to possessing her creative talent, rather than
undertake the task of developing himself in this way.

For the next example I have chosen an obscure vague
dream, that looks at first sight unlikely to fit the category of
'idealisation' dream that we are working on here. I have
done so because it shows how even a scrappy, unclear
dream — the sort you may not even bother to record — can
yield surprising and useful insights for the dreamer.

In this dream, the personal context of the dreamer, a
woman of twenty four, is most important in understanding
the powerful yet vague feelings she has towards the 'Scottish Priest'. In real life, her father had left the family when
she was one year old, and she had never seen him again.
Her mother had been unwilling or unable to talk about him,
and so the child had grown up knowing practically nothing
about this powerful missing figure in her life. She did,
however, gather that he had 'gone up North somewhere'
after leaving home.

Absent figures, whether they are distanced by death,
geography or status, are powerful symbols on which to

focus and project our idealisations of every kind; in this case, the woman was using the absent male like a blank screen to project an unknown side of herself that turned out later to have much to do with her own higher religious and spiritual aspirations. This was the dream:

> It was a very long, vague dream, very dark and confused. I'm wandering about in the darkness; I know I'm being threatened in some way by 'evil-doers' lurking about just out of sight. Nothing is clear, I don't know what I'm supposed to be doing here. I only know I must find the Scottish Priest. Just that. I don't actually ever see him, *I just know about him*. He is the only person who can help.

This is almost entirely a feeling dream, with the visual imagery limited to a dark and formless landscape in which the dreamer wanders. At one point, however, she stopped to watch the northern lights (aurora borealis), multi-coloured curtains of shifting light reflected on the low clouds. In the dream and afterwards the dreamer says that she felt this to be deeply significant, a moment of light and hope in the darkness.

Using the association exercise quickly led her to identify the man she sought as her missing father but she had no idea why he had turned into a priest, and was looking for a more suitable way of working further on this dream.

In our dreamwork, a general rule of thumb is that the more we want to understand a symbolic figure, the closer we must move towards it. Using the association exercise, for example, we move closer to the symbol through time, by restimulating our memory. We move closer still by using dream dialogue, and with daydreaming we actually step back into the dream to discover how it continues. In this next exercise the dreamer can get even more fully in touch with the essential meaning of the Dream Lover by getting inside his skin and acting out the role he represents.

The Acting Out Technique

This technique consists of re-stimulating and using in adult form yet another of our neglected infant abilities; this time it is the child's natural inclination to play 'let's pretend' games. You will immediately understand the use of this exercise if you recall the role-playing games you no doubt enjoyed as a child, when you pretended to be a nurse, pirate, detective, mother, father, and all the other personal heroes and heroines of childhood.

. As an adult you can use similar games to try out an ideal model to see how it feels. You can take any aspect of the Dream Lover that you admire or envy, and deliberately 'act out' that role, as if you were really that person yourself. This process can be both exciting and challenging, for we are likely to glimpse the wider possibilities of our self-development, whilst at the same time realising the effort and commitment required to move closer to our ideals.

Let us see what might happen if, for example, the woman whose dream is reported above were to act out the role of the absent Scottish Priest.

1 First, she would need to imagine as fully as possible what such a person would look like: how would he stand, what would be his facial expression, how would he dress, what sort of gestures would he use, would he be carrying anything?

2 Again using her imagination, she would decide what his tone of voice would be, and what sort of things such a person might say.

3 Having thus studied the role she would then act it out, by walking, talking, standing and sitting like him, getting into the part as fully as possible.

4 Once in the role, she is in a position to explore further by asking herself questions:

How does it *feel* to be a priest?

What feels better, what feels worse, compared to my normal self?

If I were him, how would I conduct my life from now on?

If I were him, how would I relate to others?

If I were him, what would be my values, ideals and priorities?

. . . and so on.

Growing Pains

There are two main ways in which we can learn from this exercise. First, we are able to get directly in touch, on a feeling level, with our ideal models, and this experience can have a powerful re-motivating effect. Perhaps our ideals are *primarily* feeling based, and we are motivated towards our aspirations by a yearning for a particular 'good feeling', which is hard to define, but which is something like joy, happiness, fulfilment. We intuitively know that being more like our ideal will make us feel more complete.

Secondly, many people find it difficult to get into this exercise at first. This resistance will give you some valuable information about yourself if you notice carefully the reasons and ideas that pop up to prevent you performing this game: 'I'm too busy, too old, too young, too stupid, too short, too feminine, too clumsy, too clever, too impatient, too weak . . . to act out my ideals.'

These very same reasons and ideas about yourself are the clues to understanding why progress towards your ideals has been hindered in the past. Going through these barriers of embarrassment, fear, self-criticism and inadequacy constitutes the growing pains of self-development.

Keeping It in Perspective

This technique is not intended in any way to encourage hypocrisy about yourself. It is not a way of covering up your authentic self with pretended virtues. I do not suggest that you can or should set out to fool or impress others by putting on an act. This is a private exercise for your own understanding, but equally, it is not designed to help you fool yourself. The acting-out technique is solely to assist you to loosen up, contradict, explore and clarify the boundaries and barriers around your own self-image.

At the very least, it will make you more tolerant of others' shortcomings, as you become more acquainted in yourself with the hard work involved in positive self-development.

CHAPTER 10

. . . AND THE BEAST'

THE DREAM LOVER IN NIGHTMARES: The Roots of Fear
— Getting Through the Fear Barrier — Inside the Blanket
Monster – Old Man Death — Facing the Beast

THE DREAM LOVER IN NIGHTMARES

At the other extreme from the over-idealised figure of the Perfect Partner is the 'Beast' of the opposite sex. In nightmares, the Dream Lover now presents us with all our worst fears and negative feelings about the opposite sex. In my professional role I sometimes hear of real-life relationships that could be fairly described as waking nightmares, in which men and women live out large periods of their lives bound to a partner who treats them badly. Yet, no matter how abusive or fearsome the partner, the victim often feels quite unable to break free from the relationship.

Just as the fantasy of the Perfect Partner can hold us spell-bound by desire, so the Beast can hold us spell-bound by fear, both in dreams and in waking life.

There are remarkable similarities between descriptions of bad relationships and the nightmares that come in the form of dreams. In both cases, the victims speak of feeling paralysed, bogged down and powerless to help themselves. People also talk of their fear of 'letting go' of a relationship, even though rationally they can see it is destructive, a situation that is reflected in dreams where we find ourselves clinging to high buildings or cliffs, in terror of falling. Oppressive, stifling feelings in the chest are common in nightmares, again echoing the claustrophobic atmosphere of relationships in which one partner feels oppressed and dominated by the other. Incidentally, these feelings can also manifest physically, in symptoms such as asthma, as the victim bottles up anxiety, fear and rage in the chest.

Powerlessness is a constant theme in nightmares, where we look on, horrified yet helpless, as some act of cruelty or violence is about to be committed on ourselves or on a loved one.

The feared figure causing these feelings in our dreams is either plainly in view, in the guise of someone threatening to shoot, eat, execute or engulf the dreamer, or may be experienced as an unknown, invisible being, whose presence is sensed as evil and hostile.

In our dream lives, we usually cope with the occasional nightmare by avoiding the issue — we simply wake up. When we find ourselves in an intolerable relationship in real life, however, many of us cope with the problem in the opposite way — we simply 'fall asleep' to some degree. This happens when we deny, ignore or suppress our true experience of the situation, burying ourselves in work, obsessive domestic chores, drink, drugs, and sometimes psychosomatic illness.

But what *is* the issue, what is the problem that we try so hard to avoid? The answer, in both dreaming and waking nightmares, is: *helpless* fear. I emphasise the word 'helpless', because there is a crucial difference between fearful situations where we feel we can do something about it, and situations where we become paralysed through a conviction of our own powerlessness.

The Roots of Fear

The roots of fear can be both widely spread and deeply

embedded in the past. We all share the fear of death, for example, and our individual life experiences can focus this basic fear in a variety of ways, such as war experience, severe emotional deprivation, accidents or serious illness, and any other dangerous and life-threatening situation. In working with your dreams you may also discover obvious and recent 'triggers' for nightmare fears, through exposure to films, books, and TV programmes featuring, for example, nuclear holocaust, rape, murder, famine, fire and the super-natural.

There is no cure for fear, in the sense that we could guarantee never to feel fearful again. We all have to live with this fact, but most of the time there will be ways of dealing with our helplessness, and it is this aspect of fear which is most promising and challenging in terms of self-development.

It is a commonplace that situations rendering one person helpless with fear may be experienced as a mild threat or a stimulating challenge by another person. We might find ourselves rigid with fear if we were trapped on a narrow cliff ledge but an experienced climber in the same position would feel much more comfortable, clear-headed and able to cope with the situation. The climber is used to facing and mastering this particular form of fear because he (or she) has deliberately trained himself to do so. He has, in other words, faced and dealt with his initial helplessness.

Helplessness is the ground in which fear finds its deepest roots, and many of our strongest and most irrational terrors stem from childhood, where we first encountered situations wherein we were indeed quite helpless, dependent and in need of protection.

One type of fear that can be firmly planted long before we reach our 'teens is fear of strong feelings, and in particular, fear of witnessing or expressing anger and sexuality.

A child's capacity to feel OK about its feelings depends almost totally on the parents' own capacity to allow and share emotions appropriately. When the parents are over-anxious, insensitive, distant, violent or simply too strict and rigid in disciplining the child's natural emotions and sensuality, then it is easy to understand how a child can come to fear and suppress its own feeling responses.

When strong feelings are suppressed, however, they do not just disappear; instead, they tend to assume distorted forms and return to us later in the guise of nightmares. Or worse, we may find ourselves acting out unresolved childhood conflicts in our adult relationships.

Forbidden fantasies of revenge, violent anger, sex and victimisation from childhood can form the basic dynamic which keeps two people locked into a relationship that is clearly unrewarding, if not plainly destructive.

This chapter will focus on inner fears, involving opposite sex figures as they appear in nightmare dreams. But I want to make it quite clear that this work, although it may be relevant, is not by itself a realistic way to tackle real-life nightmare relationships. If you are currently involved in a 'Beast and Victim' partnership, the issues to be faced will need much more practical and emotional external support. Contact your local Relate office (formerly the Marriage Guidance Council) for initial advice and help, or an independent specialist counsellor. Seek out local support groups, such as Alcoholics Anonymous or Narcotics Anonymous for skilled help in dealing with partners with drink or drug problems. Your GP or Citizens' Advice Bureau will help you contact local resources if the problem is violence in the family.

Getting Through the Fear Barrier

Nobody *likes* nightmares! Typically, we want to forget them as soon as possible. They often don't get recorded. Waking from a nightmare, instead of writing it down, the dreamer seeks immediate first aid for his anxiety, in the form of self-comforting or distraction. We will have something to eat or drink, listen to music, go for a walk, seek out someone close to comfort us. We want to distance ourselves quickly from the fear. In a while, we begin to feel better, the nightmare fades, and we thankfully get on with life. We don't want any reminders of our anxiety, and so the nightmare is forgotten, unrecorded.

Perhaps you have already encountered the Beast in the course of your dreamwork so far, and if so, I'm willing to bet that these are the dreams which you have been least able to resolve. The basic problem is this: you probably don't *want* to know what the dream was about, because the message is wrapped up in a heavy veil of fear.

This is hardly surprising. In my work I have noticed that two major themes form the core of much nightmarish material: fear of death, and fear of forbidden sexual feelings. These are also two major taboo subjects in our culture. No 'normal' person would want to explore these areas; there is a conspiracy of silence. But these are fundamental issues of life, and if we continue to turn a blind eye, it is inevitable that they will remain with us in distorted nightmare forms.

In the following two nightmare dreams you will be able to see how these taboo subjects can force themselves into awareness despite the dreamer's conscious reluctance to consider such topics.

Inside the Blanket Monster

This is the latter part of a bad dream reported by a man in his late thirties. It occurred not long after a traumatic rejection from a woman he had lived with for a year, and who had lost interest in him sexually. In the earlier part of the dream he had identified himself as a disembodied donkey's head, and he was not sure whether the head was dead or still alive. The head was sacrificed by being thrown to the Blanket Monster, lurking in the street below:

> Inside the monster, I was surprised to find opulent furnishings, sofas, beds and cushions everywhere, draped with silks and furs. I was attracted to a naked woman sprawling on a bed. I bent down to see her face, which was apparently hidden behind

a curtain but to my horror I discovered that she had no head — she was just a body.

Looking round, I now saw that the place was thronged with naked women of all kinds, and they were all headless and anonymous. I was so terrified I began to run about, desperately looking for a human face, to escape these gruesome bodies. Not just any face, I realised, but my own mother's face. I ran around helplessly, trying to call 'Mother!' but my voice had disappeared. I felt weak, and could only move in slow-motion. I couldn't find her, and around every corner was another terrifying woman's body, headless but alive.

It is difficult to overlook the marked separation of head (rational, in control) and body (unruly, sexual and mysterious) which exists within the dreamer. This symbolic separation is a common device designed unconsciously to protect us from coming to terms with the fact that we all possess a feeling, emotional and sexual side.

Marked, too, is the dreamer's flight from flagrant (headless) sexuality towards the simple, asexual innocence of childhood. But in seeking out the familiar security of his mother, it is her *face* that he wants; emphatically *not* her body. He does not want to be reminded of his mother's sexuality because this is a fearful and unresolved issue for him, reflected now, perhaps, in his recent unhappy sexual experience.

In subsequent dreamwork, looking for the focus of his fear inside the Blanket Monster (his mother's bed), this man realised that the ultimate horror would have been to have discovered her, faceless and naked like all the other women. All his life he had unconsciously turned a blind eye to her sexual nature. As I say, many of us do this, in order to avoid the uncomfortable, threatening or embarrassing fact that our parents are also sexual beings.

With great difficulty this man was able to open his eyes to the truth that his mother was a taboo yet fascinating, sexual woman, who would, quite unconsciously, have coloured and formed his own sexual awareness. The name of the Beast in this instance is incest, or rather, incestuous thoughts and feelings deeply feared and suppressed.

When we are faced with such realisations through our dreamwork, there is usually a feeling of disturbance and embarrassment, together with an urge to do something about it. But I say that there is nothing further *to* be done; facing the plain facts of our fears is its own reward, complete in itself.

The plain facts, as this man discovered, can be simply stated, something like this:

We have all had, and will continue to have, sexual feelings for all sorts of people. When these basically normal feelings are present towards members of our own family they are seen as illicit, for social and moral reasons. Therefore, we learn to control the feelings and choose not to express them in explicit sexual behaviour. But these feelings *do* need to be acknowledged to *ourselves*, otherwise we set up 'no-go areas' in our own self-awareness and risk having the feelings suppressed into the unconscious, from whence they are liable to return in more uncontrolled and fearful forms.

In the case of the example I have quoted, by being willing to work on a fearful image of the Dream Lover, the dreamer is rewarded with a simple realisation, which he can easily handle as an adult. He has de-mystified his fear of the naked, faceless women by facing the image and resolving it into a clear statement of a common human conflict.

Old Man Death

In this next dream, a fifty-year-old woman finds herself suddenly confronted by a death threat from her Dream Lover in the guise of an old man, at the end of an otherwise innocuous dream sequence:

> I was wandering about in a strange town, with no particular purpose in mind. I noticed that everywhere I went I would see the same group of young people, sometimes one or two together, sometimes more. I think there were about six of them.

91

I wasn't sure if I knew them. They always seemed on the verge of approaching me, but we never spoke. I was just aware of them, and increasingly interested, because we kept bumping into each other, in shops, in the street, and so on.

I followed one young man into a cafe. He went to the counter, and I noticed he was carrying a trombone. Then, out of the corner of my eye, I saw an old man in the street outside. He limped up to the door, slowly, helping himself along with a stick. He was dressed in old-fashioned Bohemian style, with a soft black felt hat, scarf and velvet jacket. He had dark glasses and a very white face.

His approach made me feel anxious; he seemed to have something to do with me but my attention was now drawn back to the young man at the counter, who had raised the trombone to his lips. I suddenly realised it was a plot to kill me. The young man was to play a note on the trombone to distract me and to cover the noise as the old man shot me.

I glanced back in terror at the old man. Yes, he was lifting the stick, which was a disguised gun. Desperately, I leaned to one side, trying to avoid the coming shot. The trombone sounded a loud note, and I woke up.

Death is frequently used in dreams to symbolise some form of significant and challenging change looming up in the dreamer's life. If we only knew for certain what to expect at the end of this life, I'm sure our fear of death would be much diminished. As it is, death stands as a universal symbol of the Unknown. We know that we shall all have to face this ultimate, radical change, but we won't know what it is like until we find out from experience. So the *idea* of death constellates all our other anxieties about loss, change and uncertainty in life.

The personal context of the dreamer's life situation is therefore of first importance in understanding a nightmare in which death threatens. We could ask ourselves, 'What is coming to an end in my life, and what are my fears in facing up to this change?'

In the dream quoted above, a strong clue to the central problem is that the woman's attention is focused on the young people. She is interested, but unsure of her relationship to them, and whilst she is thus distracted, 'old age' creeps up and threatens her with extinction.

We could see her dream as a dramatic reminder that, at fifty, she needs to face the painful dilemmas of middle-age which come upon us all. If we spend too much time wistfully looking back on our youth, we are apt to find that the next stage of our lives arrives unannounced, unforeseen, and in a frightening form.

Any natural change can become a crisis if we do not face up to what is going on; yet our lives seem designed to help us grow accustomed to these transitions and endings. The very process of growth can be seen as a series of 'little deaths'. Our childhood 'dies' when we enter adolescence. If we become parents, we must inevitably 'die' out of these roles when our children become independent. And our youth seems to die as we come to middle-age. Perhaps part of this, as far as our relationships are concerned, is our fear that we shall 'die' to the opposite sex when we are past our sexual prime?

Certainly, much of this was true for the woman in this case. With a divorce in the offing, she was suffering considerable bouts of depression, hopelessness and low self-esteem.

In the dream, 'Old Man Death', in the form of the Dream Lover, represents a challenge from within herself. Preoccupied with her fading youth, she was overlooking her urgent need for a period of review and re-evaluation of her personal priorities and goals. She would be wise, at this time in her life, to question herself about her present needs and expectations in her relationships; the answers could well be surprisingly different from those that served her in her previous life stage.

Unfortunately, many couples fail to realise this as they move into mid-life, and the need for review and change remains unacknowledged, buried under feelings of mutual insecurity and fear of altering a settled life-style.

Facing the Beast

It is clear from the examples we have looked at, that the chief obstacle to understanding the Dream Lover in nightmares is our natural reluctance to stand our ground and resolutely face the fearful image. We need to overcome this reluctance by remembering, recording and then exploring the unwelcome issues raised by the dream. If you can do this — and of course it is entirely up to you whether you choose to work in this area — then the battle is already half-won.

For this reason, I am not going to suggest that any one dreamwork technique is best for dealing with nightmares. Association, dream dialogue, daydreaming or acting out will all work well in bringing you to a clearer understanding of the personal issues that can occasionally turn your Dream Lover into a nightmare figure.

But I would like to introduce here a further fascinating possibility, which could greatly enhance your capacity to deal with fears without retreating into helplessness. This is not so much a technique as a concept, and the concept is this: that the dreamer can alter the ways he 'normally' acts in dreams, and resolve the issue on the spot, as it were, whilst still dreaming. This possibility exists simply because the rules are different in the dreamworld from the rules of everyday life. This obvious fact is usually forgotten while we are dreaming, which is why most of us habitually abort a nightmare when the situation becomes intolerable, by waking up.

Remember the terrifying Witch of the West in *The Wizard of Oz*? When she is finally drenched in water (feelings), she sizzles, shrinks and disappears, leaving only a pile of black clothes and a pointed hat. Essentially, there was nothing to her — it was the *costume* of fear that turned her into an image of evil.

Similarly, I am suggesting that we can take up buckets of water, heavy sticks, or any other weapon that is handy in the dream, and turn the tables on our persecutors by direct attack. We can, in dreams, give up our helpless attempts to escape and concentrate instead on defeating our fears directly and *safely* — because in the dreamworld we can never lose. We will always survive.

Thus, you can safely let go of the cliff-edge, you will survive if you are shot, you will not be killed if you turn to face the monster. Something else will happen instead, and this is likely to be a symbolic expression of renewed freedom and power. Many 'falling' dreams, for example, turn into flying dreams, much to the surprise and pleasure of the dreamer who takes the risk of letting go.

This courageous approach to nightmares is described in accounts of the Senoi people of Malaysia. In their culture, dreamwork is a highly valued and respected part of the community's everyday life. Among the Senoi, the accepted way of dealing with an adversary in a dream is to attack it and subdue it, recruiting other people in the dream to help if necessary. Once overcome, the nightmare figure will be transformed into an ally of the dreamer, who is then able to use its powers and gifts for his or her own purposes.

In our terms, we could say that the gift which comes from confronting the Dream Lover in nightmares is courage, and this is a gift that, ultimately, we give to ourselves.

CHAPTER 11

THE RIVAL

DREAMS ABOUT JEALOUSY: Deprivation and Dependency
— Separate Realities — Changing the Point of View

DREAMS ABOUT JEALOUSY

I was at a party, looking for Robert. We had arrived together, but I had lost touch with him in the crowd. Then, in a corner, I discovered a kind of transparent screen in the wall; I could see through the wall into a secret room. There was Robert. He had his back to me, but I could see *her* (Susan, his new lover), smiling up at him. They looked so close, so intimate. I couldn't stand it! I felt so jealous and hurt. But I couldn't turn away. I just stood there, suffering, until the feelings got so intense I woke up, and I was crying.

No need to wonder what such dreams are about; jealousy dreams are unmistakable. This is the Dream Lover in his cruellest form — preferring another to yourself, giving his love and attention to your rival. The feelings are so intense that we wonder how we can endure the pangs.

Oddly enough, unfounded jealousy, where we imagine our partner is up to something behind our backs, is often *more* of a mental torture (for both partners) than jealousy caused by real infidelities with a real rival as in the dream quoted above. This surely points to where the root of the jealousy problem really lies — within ourselves.

When jealousy takes hold we are said to fall into the grip of the Green-Eyed Monster, a popular expression that provides an apt metaphor for this experience. A woman once told me that she felt her jealousy as an almost physical presence in her abdomen: 'It's like a dragon or a wild dog, it eats me up.' And, significantly, she was deeply ashamed of the feeling: 'What can I *do* with it, except try to hide how I really feel?'

I asked her what part of her was being eaten up. After much thought she said, tentatively, 'My self-esteem? I feel so worthless, it must be that. I feel so bad about myself, I even feel guilty taking up people's time talking about it.'

This shame, often felt by people in the throes of jealousy, looks at first glance like a minor by-product of the central problem. But I believe it deserves much closer attention, because feelings we are ashamed of are usually the ones that keep us most helpless, tied-up and stuck. Since we are too ashamed, or too scared, to share them, we have no ready means to get them out of our system, and we cannot engage the support and reassurance of others.

Part of the extreme discomfort of being jealous is that, in itself, it is not a 'pure' feeling: rather, it is a horrible cocktail of some of the most difficult and unattractive emotions we can have — including anger, fear, grief, hurt, malice and hopeless longing. This complexity makes it harder still to share the feeling, even with sympathetic friends.

Not only are the feelings all jumbled up, they are also all 'bad' feelings, the ones we don't want, and, we are convinced, others don't want to hear about. It is a psychological truism that whenever we have a 'bad' feeling we are inclined to believe that *we* are bad, unlovable and unattractive. Self-criticism, self-blame and self-punishment can then follow, and our self-esteem can spiral downwards under the assault.

The foundations for self-assurance are laid in childhood. The key question for anyone who frequently has jealousy trouble in adult life is, therefore, 'Did you feel emotionally secure as a child?' If you lacked sufficient and constant unconditional acceptance and affection as a child, there will be some cracks in the foundations of your feelings of self-worth, and it is among these cracks that the Green-Eyed Monster lives.

As adults, when we find that we are ashamed of our jealous thoughts and malicious feelings, part of that shame is our sense of being 'too childish' and unreasonable, which is a strong clue to the origin of the trouble. Part of us *is* feeling childish but this can be a healthy urge. If we are willing, and in the right circumstances, we can let ourselves regress a little, in order to trace our troubles back to their roots and begin to deal with this unfinished business. And so, as best we can, let us face the Monster in its lair.

As a first step we might look more closely at the cocktail of feelings which makes up our jealousy. I would say that some of them are expected healthy adult responses to loss. When a lover has been lost to a rival, it's a real loss: we have lost a source of love, attention, interest, support and general emotional security. *Naturally* we feel grief at the loss; naturally we fear 'What will become of me now?' and naturally we feel angry: 'How dare he (or she) do this to me?'

There is no more reason to be ashamed of these feelings than there is to feel wrong about the emotional upset of losing a partner through bereavement. If the feelings are freely expressed and accepted, time will heal the loss.

Every loss has the potential to stir up past experiences that produced similar feelings. If these past situations have not been adequately dealt with and let go, we find ourselves stuck in mental fantasies of spiteful revenge, nursed grudges, schemes to 'get even'. To a large extent, we are then re-living times when, as a powerless child unfairly wronged, we railed bitterly at the injustice of life. No wonder we want to draw a veil of shame over this aspect of our jealousy.

All forms of jealousy challenge our ability and willingness to let go of the past, but if you find yourself frequently and obsessively dwelling on past hurts and injustices, in your thoughts or in your dreams, really letting go may require sustained and determined efforts on your part. In such a case, therefore, I would recommend seeking an individual counsellor to help in the work of releasing and dealing with these ties to the past.

If, however, your feelings of jealousy are less frequent and more tolerable, you can make much progress by working directly on building up and strengthening your own foundation of self-esteem.

Deprivation and Dependency

The two personality traits which do most to undermine both men and women's good feelings about themselves, making them prone to possessiveness and jealousy, are deprivation and dependency.

A deep-seated feeling of deprivation can be set up early in life if the parents are niggardly with affection, time and attention. The child can feel neglected, left short of love, if they are too distant — emotionally, mentally or physically — around the home, or too distant in reality, as when children are farmed out before they are ready, to relatives or a boarding school. As an adult with such a background, you may still feel needy, hungry for affection and care, and looking primarily to others to fill these needs.

Lingering feelings of dissatisfaction in relationships, and jealous, possessive thoughts, stem from the basic inner conviction of the deprived person, which is: 'I will never get enough affection.' This conviction overlooks the possibility of developing affection for yourself; as an adult you now have great resources and endless opportunities to fill any deficit of care from the past by directly and personally ministering more to your own needs.

Begin to treat yourself with the respect and attention that you *would* deserve *if* you were a worthy and highly esteemed individual! Begin to love and look after yourself in all the ways you have been wishing others would in the past, by taking care of your diet, exercise and general health, by allowing yourself generous gifts of theatre visits, clothes, books, flowers, a massage, a holiday in the sun, and so on. You know what you want to be given, so begin to give it to yourself.

Patterns of dependency, too, originate in childhood. In this case, the parents are too attentive and preoccupied with the child's care. 'Wrapped in cotton wool' the child is hardly allowed to do anything for him- or herself and the natural urge towards growing independence is constantly thwarted, even in the teens and twenties. After years of learning that everything depends on others doing it for you, the dependent adult will cling desperately and jealously to any and every partner, for the inner conviction here is, 'I am useless on my own.'

If you feel anything like this, remind yourself now that you have no real idea of what you are 'worth' by yourself, because you have never seriously tried to find out! For you, the untapped potential for your self-esteem lies in giving priority to those projects which are done best by playing or working or exploring alone. Redecorate a room without asking anyone's advice or help; replan and replant a corner of the garden all by yourself. Read and research into a subject that interests you alone, not something that someone else has suggested. Spend at least one whole day a week alone, without a fixed schedule, and give yourself time to think out and explore new projects you could do alone. Try out some solitary sports and pastimes, such as fishing, hiking, painting, or writing poetry.

These are the sorts of things that will encourage and develop your pride in your own abilities and achievements, to the point where you no longer tell yourself how useless you are, but rather can point to a growing list of good experiences achieved alone and unaided. This store of inner esteem will eventually become a reliable resource to help free you from the immobilising grip of jealousy and over-dependence on others.

Separate Realities

All the problems of jealousy are related in some way to the ease or difficulty with which we can handle separation, or rather, how well we respond to the fact that each person is essentially a complete separate individual, living a separate life, with his or her separate reality. We all have much in common, and can recognise, share and enjoy each other's experiences in life, but nevertheless, each person's life is ultimately about that person, and no-one else.

The experience of jealousy, in reality or in fantasies and dreams, is based on the mistaken belief that other people's lives must always be about us: then, 'of course Robert fell in love with Susan to hurt me, and of course Susan lured Robert away from me because she hates me and is envious of me. And of course they flaunt their relationship in public to humiliate me. They want to make me feel worthless and small,' and so on.

If this dreamer really liked herself, if she truly enjoyed her own life for her own sake, jealousy would find little space in which to root. As it is though, she feels victimised. She allows the way they lead their lives to be the cause of her discomfort, rather than attending to her own wobbly self-confidence.

Changing the Point of View

It is ironic that habitually jealous people derive much of their suffering from a personal asset which could instead be a source of great enjoyment, liberation and creativity — their imaginations. Despite themselves, they find they can only use their imaginations to give themselves a bad time. Fantasy scenes and dialogues, featuring 'Them' together, with 'Me' excluded and despised, provide an exquisitely painful, but seductive and compelling form of self-torture.

The trouble with our dreamer is that she cannot stop

thinking about 'them' as if everything they did, thought and felt was about her, and directed at her.

In this next technique, therefore, I am going to suggest a different way of employing your imagination. Using the sample dream described at the beginning of the chapter, I invite you to re-write it from the point of view of first Robert, and then Susan.

Use your creative powers to put yourself into their shoes, and describe how they feel, what their thoughts and pre-occupations might be, what they might say to each other at the party, what their lives in general might be about. You can make up stories about their past, their future individual plans, their fears, worries, hopes and ideals. There is only one rule: nothing you write must refer directly or indirectly to the dreamer, the 'jealous one'.

You may object that this is a waste of time, because the figures in the sample dream are nothing to do with you personally, but this is just the point, for the next step is to re-write a jealousy dream of your own, in which you *are* personally involved, in the same way: from the point of view of the 'miscreants' who are 'hurting' you, but excluding all reference to yourself.

The exercise will show you precisely how difficult it is to unravel the mental and emotional identifications, to let go of a relationship, and to exorcise the jealous conviction that others lead their lives to spite you.

As I said at the beginning of this chapter, the Dream Lover appears in a cruel form when we experience jealousy dreams, but despite the pain of such dreams, they can be seen as doing us a service, for jealousy reminds us of a need to re-assess and repair our general self-confidence and satis-faction with life.

If we can then confront the Green-Eyed Monster in the ways I have suggested, rather than remaining its helpless victim, we can emerge from the struggle stronger and more confident in ourselves.

CHAPTER 12

BECOMING YOUR OWN COUNSELLOR

SEEING THE DREAMER IN THE DREAM: Focusing on the Dreamer — What the Dreamer Does — What the Dreamer Feels — What the Dreamer Believes — Prompting Statements — How the Dreamer Could Change — Does It Ring True?

SEEING THE DREAMER IN THE DREAM

When we observe other couples (or gossip about them with mutual friends!) it is surprisingly easy to spot the rights and wrongs of their behaviour, and to come up with simple clear advice on what they should or should not be doing about it. Unfortunately, it is not so easy to step outside our own relationships to see with the same degree of clarity and detachment what we are up to.

We are usually too involved to get this overview of ourselves. What is more, we frequently lose sight of our own actions because we are strongly focused on trying to alter our partners' behaviour in some way.

Whatever we learn about ourselves and how we act within relationships tends to come with hindsight, maybe years after we have left a particular partner, when it is far too late to make any difference. These delayed insights are of great value but the problem remains that, while we are waiting for the penny to drop, we may be repeating patterns of unconscious behaviour that simply do not work well for us, and which may actively prevent us from gaining the satisfaction we seek in our relationships.

In contrast to this, our relationships with the Dream Lover are always with us, constantly available as part of our self-learning process. Our work so far in Part Two has been largely concerned with techniques to help us look more closely at the Dream Lover. In this chapter, however, we will attempt to shift the focus, from what the Dream Lover does in the dream to how we ourselves act, or fail to act. This can be a difficult feat, for in our dreamlives and in subsequent dreamwork we are always prone to become over-involved, and lose our objectivity.

What we need is an approach that will enable us to assume the role of our own 'counsellor', with a more objective overview of our actions, feelings and attitudes as mirrored in the dream. We will then be in a better position to notice, and comment upon, *both* sides of the Dream Lover relationship, for it is easy to forget that, in dreams as in waking life, it takes two people to make a relationship the way it is. Whether you are interacting with your Dream Lover or with a real-life partner, you are 'the other half', and the way that you relate will contribute greatly to the pleasure or pain that the relationship brings you.

Focusing on the Dreamer

The first step in this new approach is to drop the word 'I' when you write down your dream, and substitute a more objective description — the Dreamer. This I have done in the following sample dream, which we will be using later to illustrate how the technique works in practice. The dreamer in this case is a divorced man in his forties:

> The Dreamer has to meet his twelve-year-old son at a radio station, but cannot find it. He is lost in a strange town, and worried about time passing. The Dreamer runs from woman to woman, hoping they will understand what he wants, which is

to be reunited with his little boy. But he is so confused and panicky he doesn't seem to have time to express himself clearly, nor can he make any sense of what the women in the dream are saying and doing.

All of the dozen or so people encountered by the Dreamer are women. [Just three of these figures have been selected here, in order to keep the dream of manageable length for the exercise.]

He finds himself in a high-class brothel, in a special room. He understands that in this room the clients may do whatever it is that they find sexually obsessive. A woman seductively suggests that the Dreamer helps her to rub some ointment into her eyebrow, because she has an inflamed eye. The Dreamer is embarrassed and puzzled, yet finds it difficult to say that he is not interested. Eventually, he manages to slip out through a side door, where he finds himself back in the strange town and lost again . . .

He then meets a woman with four hands bunched in the centre of her chest. He thinks: 'She is a thalidomide victim,' and is too shocked to ask her clearly for help. So he simply shouts at her, 'Just point me in the right direction,' without further explanation. The woman is hurt and resentful. 'You reject my energy,' she says. 'I would have sent you energy through your apron strings.' And as he hurries off to continue his search, the Dreamer discovers that he is wearing an apron over his evening dress . . .

At long last, the Dreamer finds a cafe in the foyer of what he hopes is the radio station. He approaches a waitress, a plain woman in her early forties, dressed in a beige nylon overall and cap. He asks if she has seen his son. 'He's all right,' she says, off-hand and busy with her coffee machine. The Dreamer is still not sure, and harasses her until she consults another waitress, and then tells the Dreamer, 'He is safe in another room.' The Dreamer relaxes at last, asks for some coffee and cake, and wakes up.

Having written out our dream in this manner we can consider it as if it were a story about *someone else's* relationship with the opposite sex. By temporarily disassociating ourselves from the Dreamer we are better able to bring our objectivity to bear, because we have an overview of the situation between our friend the Dreamer and his Dream Lover.

Taking up the role of counsellor we can now systematically observe, analyse and advise the Dreamer. In the following sections we will use our sample dream to focus in turn upon: What the Dreamer *does*, what the Dreamer *feels*, what the Dreamer *believes* and finally, how the Dreamer could *change*.

Stage 1: What the Dreamer Does

Look back through the dream-story and write down whatever you observe of the Dreamer's actions or activities.

Thus you might see that:

The Dreamer runs about from woman to woman in a great hurry.

He does not take time to collect his thoughts.

He has difficulty in expressing his needs clearly to the women.

He does not have time to listen to the women properly.

He acts impulsively, starting out to search at random, even though he does not know the area, nor the right direction.

He frequently loses himself.

. . . and so on.

You might also find it helpful to construct a more generalised statement about the Dreamer's active role in the dream, such as, 'He searches for an important part of himself, but is distracted by the women he meets and hampered by his lack of knowledge in this area.'

You will notice that the absence of actions and responses that would be appropriate in real life is also significant. The Dreamer in this example does *not* take time to orientate himself; he does *not* clearly state what he wants (until the last encounter); he does *not* express his embarrassment and puzzlement in the brothel. This is an important point because in many dreams the Dreamer seems to be nothing more than a disembodied eye, receiving impressions without response, like a camera, but in such dreams the

Dreamer *is* 'doing something' — he is remaining passive; he is withholding his reaction and interaction when confronted by the Dream Lover, and immediately the question arises, 'Is this how he is with his real-life partners — passive, unresponsive, uninvolved?'

Stage 2: What the Dreamer Feels

Again, looking back over the sample dream, write a list of the Dreamer's feelings in response to the situation. Your list may look something like this:

The Dreamer feels under pressure to hurry.

He feels anxious and worried about his little boy.

He feels frustrated by, and rather threatened by the cripple and the prostitute.

He feels insecure because he keeps getting lost.

He feels irritated by the women he meets, because they do not immediately (intuitively?) understand what he wants.

He feels grief and loss at being separated from that part of himself represented by his lost child.

He feels reassured, and more trusting, when he finally meets the waitress.

Stage 3: What the Dreamer Believes

Having listed the explicit actions of the Dreamer and his feeling responses to the women he meets in the dream, we can now put these together and deduce something of his underlying attitudes and assumptions about various aspects of the opposite sex.

In this particular dream excerpt the Dream Lover presents three different aspects of herself. She is in turn:

A prostitute — one who trades on her sexuality
A handicapped victim — damaged from birth
A waitress — one who serves and feeds others.

107

At this point we need to remember that the Dream Lover is always fundamentally the same 'person': she (or he) represents the unconscious opposite of the Dreamer's conscious identity and gender. The guises in which she appears are unconsciously selected by the Dreamer, because he needs to look more closely at these aspects of his 'other half' in order to learn more about himself and his relationships.

Bearing this in mind, let us run together all three different women in the dream so as to construct a broad picture of what the Dreamer believes women to be. The initial statement, then, might go something like this, 'Women will make me pay for my sexual needs; women are born different and handicapped from birth; ideally, women will serve and nurture me.'

These are his beliefs as reflected by the three female figures in the dream, each symbolising a different aspect of his overall attitude towards women. These are just some of the unconscious preconceptions our friend will bring into his relationships with real-life partners. This is why the inner work we do with our Dream Lover is so important to our outer relationships: it is essential to become more conscious of our deeper attitudes and expectations if we hope to make positive and realistic changes in our outlook.

Prompting Statements

Another way of uncovering the Dreamer's unconscious beliefs is to use a prompting statement, such as, 'The Dreamer acts towards these women *as if* he believed they . . .' or, 'The Dreamer's feelings towards these women show that he believes they . . .' You can then fill in the blanks to complete the statements from an objective point of view.

For example, 'The Dreamer acts as if he believed women will distract and impede him; that women won't be of much practical help; that women won't understand what he wants.'

It could also be said that the Dreamer acts as if he is not actually interested in meeting and relating to women. They are merely incidental to his getting what he really wants — comfort for his child. Also, we may notice, the Dreamer acts throughout the dream as if *he* were a lost twelve-year-old!

Looking now at his feelings, we could come up with statements like, 'The Dreamer's feelings towards these women show that he believes they are sexually puzzling and embarrassing; he believes that women are intrinsically handicapped and in need of care, and that this threatens him; he believes that women have power over him "through their apron strings"; he believes that women are confused and irritating — at one juncture he has to shout to make himself understood, as if he were talking to a fool or a foreigner; he believes that women, not men, are responsible for the care and safety of little boys. On the other hand, he believes that when a boy is separated from a woman's nurturing care he is endangered.'

How the Dreamer Could Change

It is time now to don your mantle of wisdom and step into the counsellor's role, to evaluate what has been gathered about the Dreamer's beliefs — to decide which of these beliefs will enhance and foster his relationships with women, and which will tend to interfere with and frustrate his attempts to relate to the opposite sex.

On the positive side, you could say that the Dreamer values and respects women for the caring nurturing roles they can fill, namely the stereotyped mother figure or supportive wife. However, he may be far from acknowledging his own dependency on women for nurture, preferring instead to project these needs onto the child of his marriage. This belief needs to be reconsidered, too, in terms of the degree of nurturing and caring he can himself provide for a child, and for an adult partner.

When the counsellor turns to the obvious negative traits

in the Dreamer, the list is, unfortunately, a long one.

Take for example his idea that women will not understand what he wants. This is a fundamental fear frequently expressed by both men and women, that the opposite sex, because they are 'different', cannot or will not ever fully comprehend one's needs, or understand one's point of view. Often, this frustration arises not because a partner is too stupid or too malicious to hear what is being asked for but because we ourselves are not clear what we want, and /or do not express what we want clearly and unequivocally.

This factor is operating throughout the dream we have been considering and we can see how easily the Dreamer frustrates himself by not letting the women know the root cause of his anxiety. The counsellor might then wonder whether this man has ever said to a woman, 'Sometimes I feel just like a little, lost boy, and what I need from you is comfort and reassurance that you care.' The chances are, surely, that she would then understand and respond?

And what about the Dreamer's notion that 'Women will make me pay for sex'? Again, women could, and frequently do, make the same complaint of men. Women generally *are* expected to repay a man in a sexual relationship, not in money, although many women do in fact provide financial support for men, but in terms of loving care, attention, loyalty, devotion and general nurturing. Here too the counsellor could give some sound advice to the Dreamer, to reconsider whether the payments in his relationships are indeed all unilateral and unfair exchanges.

Does It Ring True?

In this manner, the Dreamer's beliefs and attitudes towards the opposite sex can be examined one by one, and reconsidered from the objective viewpoint. The last task is to put what we have learned into perspective. Remember when you perform this exercise on one of your own dreams that *you* are the Dreamer, and so whatever you deduce about

110

yourself needs to be weighed up in the context of your own life situation. After completing the exercise on your own dream, therefore, look again at the story of your patterns of relationships over the past few years: does what you have gleaned from this work ring true for you? What is important, what is less important, and what do you feel like changing?

Here is the story of the Dreamer whose dream we have been following throughout this chapter, revised and reinterpreted in the light of his dreamwork on this and other recent dreams:

> Four years after my divorce I still find myself running from woman to woman, acting and feeling like the lost little boy in the dream. I've been so angry with them; none of them seemed willing or able to make me feel better. My dreams have made me realise that my main problem has been my unwillingness to admit even to myself how needy and insecure I've been. It's not easy for a man of my age to confess to feeling like a twelve-year-old boy again.

This Dreamer had come to realise the depth of emotional security he had invested in his fifteen-year marriage. After the divorce, although on the surface he was in many ways doing well, a deeper feeling of loss was at work, restimulating unresolved issues of dependency, loneliness and fear of not being able to cope unsupported in the world, which dated back to his early adolescence.

He is, on the simplest level, feeling acutely insecure and uncared for because he still has need for a Mother figure for safety, reassurance and nurture, — and in the dream he finds such a figure, in the form of the plain, ordinary waitress.

The handicapped woman looks to him as if *she* needs to be cared for; he finds himself wearing the apron, and he feels threatened by this implicit role reversal. He is the needy one, and in this state he will tend to avoid women who want to depend on him.

The prostitute shows him that his insecurity has regressed him back beyond puberty, and that, for the time being, he is more embarrassed than interested in the sexual side of relationships.

* * *

The 'objective counsellor' technique which we have been exploring in this chapter concludes the work of Part Two.

By working through the various dreamwork exercises presented in this section, I hope you will have discovered at least some ways and means that will encourage you to go on with the investigation of your own Dream Lover material. In the process, two important questions are likely to have occurred to you repeatedly. The first is, 'Where did all these ideas I have about the opposite sex come from?' and the second, 'How can I change?'

The following two sections of the book are designed to assist you in discovering your own answers to these questions.

PART THREE
DISCOVERY

CHAPTER 13

WHERE DO DREAM LOVERS COME FROM?

HOW TO ASSEMBLE A SEXUAL INDENTIKIT: The Past: Mother and Father — Questionnaire 1: Mother — Questionnaire 2: Father — The Past: Extended Family — The Past: Brothers and Sisters — The Present: Important Adult Relationships — Questionnaire 3: Specific Adult Partner(s) — Questionnaire 4: Generally Speaking — The Cultural Input — Later Life

HOW TO ASSEMBLE A SEXUAL IDENTIKIT

We all carry within us a set of preconceptions, amounting to a kind of sexual Identikit, about what it means to be a Man, or a Woman. Discovering and acknowledging these largely unconscious ideas is the main part of the work in achieving more satisfactory relationships with the opposite sex.

Our analysis of the Dream Lover has shown us that working on our own dreams can be of crucial assistance in bringing to awareness our deep, unquestioned assumptions about gender roles. But we can greatly enhance our work in this area by systematically reviewing the sources of our sexual preconceptions, which lie buried in our personal histories.

This chapter offers a format for such a review. It comprises a series of self-questions which will enable you to research and assemble much of the raw material out of which we construct our images and ideas about sexual identity. These questionnaires are not like the familiar personality quiz or psychological test you might find in a magazine. There are no right or wrong answers and there is no score to prove or disprove anything about you.

In the following sections you will be invited to focus in turn upon root experiences at the beginning of your life: the gender models offered by parents, the wider family, teachers, etc.; then to examine your personal experiences of the opposite sex as an adult; and finally, to consider what fantasies and expectations you have about the future, what is significant about being a man or a woman in later life.

I recommend that you allow yourself plenty of time to reflect fully on each issue raised. It is worth spending a little time each day over this review, or perhaps an hour or so each week, for half-forgotten memories often take a while to emerge fully into consciousness. If you keep written notes of your ponderings you will find these an invaluable source of reference and deeper understanding as you work on your dreams and on your real life relationships.

The questions that follow raise the kind of issue that you might be asked to look at in an awareness or sexuality workshop; certainly, as an individual counsellor, I would regard this information as a basic necessity for anyone troubled by relationship problems.

This is not, however, a psychological textbook: I do not intend to present a complete theory of how your personal unconscious is constructed. I hope instead to offer the average reader an interesting exercise that will reveal some pointers to the ways one's upbringing can form and colour the archetypal opposite sex figures that appear in our dreams as the Dream Lover, and which also influence our real life relationships.

The Past: Mother and Father

There are two sets of questions printed below, one headed 'Mother' and one 'Father', and you are invited to fill out these questionnaires solely from your own knowledge and experience of these two primary gender models.

If your natural mother or father was absent from an early age, through death, desertion, divorce, etc., apply the questionnaire to any adult of the right sex who acted as a substitute for one or other parent in your life.

This person might be a foster-parent, step-parent, a lover of your single parent, grand-parent, aunt, uncle, and sometimes even an older brother or sister. What we are looking for are the people in your childhood who filled the roles, even temporarily, of the most important man and woman in your world, your parents.

Questionnaire 1: Mother

Note: Depending on your age now and on whether your parents are still alive, you will probably have modified your perceptions of your parents as you have grown more adult. If this is the case, answer the questionnaire in terms of how you related to your parents up until the time you left home. First impressions last longest, and so concentrate mostly on how your parents were to you as a child.

1 Start by writing a brief description of Mother, a character sketch in a few words. What of her appearance, 'style', health, interests, work, mental ability, emotional life, spiritual aspirations; what was her greatest joy in life? Her greatest disappointment?

2 What was her attitude towards your father; men in general; people in general?

3 What did she generally tell you to do or not to do? What do you think she expected you to be?

4 What did you like and dislike most about her?

5 What was 'missing' in her that your father had to supply?

6 Because she was a woman she couldn't . . .
Because she was a woman she could . . .

7 If I met a woman like her now, I'd tell her . . .

8 By her behaviour, mother taught me that women are . . .

9 By her behaviour, mother taught me that men are . . .

10 She didn't understand . . . about me.

11 She didn't understand . . . about men.

12 I'll never forget the time when she . . .

13 I'll never forget the time when she failed to . . .

14 Was your mother a 'real' woman, or not? Why?

15 How did she treat your brothers and sisters differently from you?

16 In what ways do you think you understood her better than your father did?

17 Was she weak or strong? In what ways?

18 Was she generally happy or unhappy with her life? Why?

19 What do you still 'owe' her? What does she still owe you?

20 I could never get close to her because . . .
She was always too close to me because . . .

21 How was she the opposite of father? How was she the same?

22 She thought that sex was . . .

23 She always said that men were . . .

24 She believed that . . . was unmanly.
She believed that . . . was unfeminine.

25 When you reached puberty, did her attitudes towards you change? In what ways? What did you take this to mean?

Questionnaire 2: Father

1 Again, start with a brief character sketch, describing Father's appearance, 'style', health, interests, work, mental ability, emotional life, spiritual aspirations; what was his greatest joy in life? His greatest disappointment?

2 What was his attitude towards your mother? Women in general? People in general?

3 What did he generally tell you to do or not to do? What do you think he expected of you?

4 What did you like and dislike most about him?

5 What was missing in him that your mother had to supply?

6 Because he was a man, he couldn't . . .
Because he was a man, he could . . .

7 If I met a man like him now, I'd tell him . . .

8 By his behaviour, father taught me that men are . . .

9 By his behaviour, father taught me that women are . . .

10 He didn't understand . . . about me.

11 He didn't understand . . . about women.

12 I'll never forget the time when he . . .

13 I'll never forget the time when he failed to . . .

14 Was your father a 'real' man or not? Why?

15 How did he treat your brothers and sisters differently from you?

16 In what ways do you think you understood him better than your mother did?

17 Was he weak or strong? In what ways?

18 Was he generally happy or unhappy with his life? Why?

19 What do you still 'owe' him? What does he still 'owe' you?

20 I could never get close to him because . . .
He was always too close to me because . . .

21 How was he the opposite of mother? How was he the same?

22 He thought that sex was . . .

23 He always said that women were . . .

24 He believed that . . . was unmanly.
He believed that . . . was unfeminine.

25 When you reached puberty, did his attitudes towards you change? In what ways? What did you take this to mean?

The Past: The Extended Family

Every adult with a significant relationship to the child inevitably contributes his or her ideas and attitudes about gender differences to the child's unconscious sexual Identikit.

120

These inputs are the root material, accepted unthinkingly as true, which the child uses to construct his or her inner picture of what it means to be male or female. And unless in later life we re-examine the models we received so uncritically as children, they will hinder and confuse us in our search for a fuller, more personal sexual identity.

So I would encourage you to do a thorough job, and recall each of the following figures in turn, asking yourself in each case, 'How did this person's attitudes contradict or confirm my parents' views?'

Both set of grandparents
Aunts, uncles and older cousins
Ex-officio members of your family, such as family friends, close neighbours
School teachers, especially at primary school.

Each of these will have contributed not only to your ideas about how to be a human being but also how to be a male or female, and how the two sexes should behave towards each other.

Furthermore, the impressionable child is exposed to the family's own inner conflicts and uncertainties about gender. The unfortunate child is often in the position of captive audience, witnessing a life-long power struggle between Mother and Father, which could sow the seeds of an insoluble 'War of the Sexes', coming to fruit in the child's own adult life.

Other members of a family can be roped in by the parents to support their own positions, and children find themselves being warned that they are in danger of turning out to be 'just like Uncle Jack', i.e. 'bad'. In just one case I know of, Uncle Jack's alleged promiscuity was used by a dominating mother to warn her adolescent son away from flirting with girls. As a result, he is still a virgin at forty, still living with his parents, and quite impossibly shy and nervous about women.

The Past: Brothers and Sisters

The gender games, and in some cases one might almost say 'gender wars', which go on below the surface in many families, can be greatly complicated by the ways that parents react to their children of either sex; between brothers and sisters there can be fierce competition to win the most affection from Mother or Father.

1 *If you were an only child,* it is worth looking back to see if there was any hint of disappointment in either parent's behaviour towards you, because you were the wrong sex! Many adult women that I have counselled have been quite sure that one or both their parents really wanted a boy, and many men have picked up subliminal messages in childhood that the parents had been wishing for a girl.

While you are pondering this, you might also like to consider why it was that you were the only child; compare the reasons your parents may have given you with your own more intuitive deductions. Many an adult, looking back on a single childhood, has told me that, just by watching what went on between the parents, it was obvious that their sex life ended with the birth of that first baby.

2 *If you grew up in an 'all boys' or 'all girls' family,* consider how you might have competed for Mother or Father's affection and approval. The strategies we develop as children to court the love of the opposite sex parent are often transferred unaltered into our adult relationships: as an adult, how do you now react when you believe there is a rival for your loved one's attention? Do you feel about them as you did when you were competing with your brothers or sisters? Finally, which of your brothers, or which of your sisters, won. That is to say, which of you managed to be Mummy or Daddy's favourite? And how did he or she achieve this?

Another frequent pattern found in families where all the children are of the same sex, is that all the sons, plus Father, gang up against Mother to exclude her from the all-male club and power-base. A similar thing can happen when all the daughters plus Mother form a united front to manage and control the only male in the household — Father. Can you remember anything like this in your own childhood?

3 *If you formed half of a 'pigeon pair'*, one boy and one girl child, your parents were probably rather satisfied with the arrangement. Modern couples tend to regard one of each, or perhaps two of each, as just about the right size and gender mix for a family.

However, just think for a moment how convoluted the gender games can become in such a family. The boy may perceive Father as a sexual role model *and* an ally against sister and Mother, *and* a rival for Mother's affection. The girl may have the same mixture of alliance and competition with her mother. Moreover there may be a tacit agreement between the parents that the boy is 'Father's' and the girl is 'Mother's', and will resist and resent each other's interference in these gender alliances.

There is ample room, too, for either child to betray his or her natural ally of the same sex, and become the classic daddy's girl or mummy's boy.

I am not of course suggesting that all or any of these overtones are present in every family but I hope you will consider whether any of these brief notes rings a bell in your own childhood memories, and if so, whether you are still engaged in similar gender games — or wars — in your adult relationships.

The Present: Important Adult Relationships

I have attempted to construct a fresh questionnaire to help you survey your current attitudes towards, and experience of, the opposite sex, so that you can compare your adult sources of Dream Lover material with the preconceptions laid down in childhood and adolescence. Depending on your age and stage of life, however, you may have had fewer or greater numbers of significant relationships as an adult; you may have had only one partner, you may not have a partner now, and so on.

Bearing in mind, then, that all the questions may not apply to you personally, I suggest you apply the questionnaire to as few or as many relationships as you wish, choosing for yourself which partnerships were most important in your life.

Questionnaire 3: Specific Adult Partner(s)

1 did you feel secure in this relationship? How did he/she make you feel secure . . . insecure . . .?

2 What was the most important thing that he/she provided?

3 What was the most important thing missing from this relationship?

4 With hindsight, can you see any strengths or weaknesses in your partner that are similar to strengths or weaknesses in your parents?

5 Was he/she stronger or better than you? Weaker or worse than you? In what respects?

6 Which of you needed the other more? Why? How did you feel about that?

7 Because I was with him/her, I felt obliged to . . . and never to . . .

8 Because he/she was 'mine', I naturally expected him/her to . . . and never to . . .

9 I was prepared to sacrifice . . . for his/her sake.

10 If I had ever done or said . . . that would have spelt the end of the relationship.

11 If he/she had ever done or said . . . that would have been the end.

12 My greatest satisfaction with this partner was . . .

13 My greatest disappointment with this partner was . . .

14 One thing I could never mention was . . .

15 One thing he/she would never discuss was . . .

16 Most of our arguments were about . . . because . . .

17 With him/her, I wish I could have been more . . . and less . . .

18 The relationship ended because my partner was . . . and wasn't . . .

19 The relationship ended because I was . . . and wasn't . . .

After you have been through this questionnaire to review what you have learned from specific adult partners, you can use the following questions to help clarify your current general attitudes and assumptions about the opposite sex.

Questionnaire 4: Generally Speaking

1 My adult experiences with the opposite sex have taught me that men are . . . and women are . . .

2 My ideal man/woman would be . . . and would not be . . .

3 I hate men/women who . . .

4 Men/women who . . . frighten me, because I can't . . .

5 One good thing about men/women is . . .

6 If I were of the opposite sex, I would . . . and I would feel more . . .

7 I would never have a . . . for a partner because . . .

8 I would never . . . for any man/woman.

9 I do/do not want children because . . .

10 I could never live alone because . . .

11 I could never live with a partner because . . .

12 I need the opposite sex for . . .

13 I do not need the opposite sex for . . .

14 I am afraid that the opposite sex thinks that I am too . . . and not . . . enough to merit their love, and this makes me feel . . .

15 I've never met a man/woman that I've wanted a long-term relationship with because they are always too . . . and are never . . . enough, and this makes me feel . . .

16 Is there anything about you that only a man/only a woman would understand?

The Cultural Input

1 If you have a religion, what does it teach or imply about how men and women differ in nature?

2 In your job or profession, what attitudes towards men/women are implied or required?

3 Is there a career or profession that you would like to try for yourself but feel you can't because you are the wrong sex? What do you feel about this? What could you do about this?

4 Was your secondary school mixed, or single sex? How did this affect your attitudes towards the opposite sex?

5 Who is your favourite fantasy partner? Which of his/her qualities do you find most attractive?

6 Is there a popular figure of your own sex that you hero-worship, envy or admire? What are the qualities in him/her that you would most like to possess?

7 The men and women portrayed in advertisements are carefully designed to give you specific ideas about the nature of men and women. Do the ideas projected through the medium of advertising generally match your own experience of the two sexes?

8 Outside of your intimate partnerships, are most of your friends of your own sex, or the opposite sex? Why do you think this is so?

Later Life

Our future expectations will inevitably influence our current choices and behaviour. We are all to some extent 'planning now' to avoid whatever problems, or to gain whatever rewards, the future seems to hold for us. The following section, therefore, invites you to focus more clearly on your picture of how later life will be for you, in terms of your gender.

1 Once I am over . . . years old, I'll lose . . . and I'll gain . . . because I am a man/woman.

2 Nobody expects men/women over . . . years old to . . .

3 Women live longer than men on average, because they are . . . and men are . . .

4 Men/women over . . . years old are . . . and they can't . . .

5 As I get older, my relationships with men/women will . . .

6 I am determined not to end up like Mother/Father because . . .

7 I welcome/I avoid contact with older men/women because . . .

8 How do you imagine your relationship with your current partner — or with some future partner — will be, in later life?

9 Finally, ask yourself: Where did I get these ideas from? Must they inevitably apply to my own life? Will I fulfil the predictions of my parental family and/or the general cultural expectation, or can I live out my life in my own unique way, despite my gender identity?

CHAPTER 14

'WHAT ABOUT ME?'

*THE SELF WITHIN THE GENDER ROLE: The Self and the
Need to Adapt — Projection: The Disowning Pattern —
Introjection: The Brainwashed Pattern — Retroflection: The
Self-blaming Pattern — Assimilation: The Pattern Breaker*

THE SELF WITHIN THE GENDER ROLE

Our work with the Dream Lover so far has been largely
concerned with psychological archaeology. Using dreamwork techniques and the historical review in the previous
chapter, we have been digging our way deeper into the
past, unearthing a growing collection of memories, associations and images that had been buried in the less accessible
parts of our minds.

All this material is an invaluable source of insight and
understanding, and can throw much light on our present
attitudes and difficulties in relation to the opposite sex.

But in digging up and assembling the various com-
ponents of our historical Dream Lover, we are not just
dealing with something lifeless and fixed by the past. We
have a living and dynamic relationship with the Dream
Lover in our dreams, and it is constantly capable of being
added to, modified and reshaped in our everyday interactions with the men and women in our world. In so far as we
are able to let go of fixed concepts about gender identity,

allowing the Dream Lover to develop and grow, we also enable ourselves to develop and grow.

I want to emphasise the point that the Dream Lover relationship is open-ended and dynamic, carrying great potential for self-development, because you may well be feeling rather buried under the mass of historical data we have been gathering. You may be wondering, 'Where do *I* come into all this? Am I just a passenger in life, framed by a sexual identity formed by my personal background?' On the contrary, I believe this is far from being the case. This chapter is designed to help you change focus, from *what* you have received from the past, to *how* you deal with it. We can't alter the past, but we can understand how past situations shaped our habitual responses or patterns in relationships, and we *can* change these patterns.

The Self and the Need to Adapt

When I refer to the 'self' in relation to the Dream Lover, I mean the central identity, the core person of which the gender identity forms just one of several more superficial aspects. In our 'selves' we are the essence of simplicity. All of us want to survive, and we are all born with a need for love, for acceptance as we are, and with an inner urge to achieve our fullest human potential.

Life, though, requires us to be rather more complicated! We have to 'be' a man or a woman, and also have to assume other important aspects of identity. Religion, class, politics and career, for example, can all require us to adapt our simple central self, and act out roles within these spheres.

The pressure to conform to a gender identity is just one way that we are 'framed' by the world in which we find ourselves. Nevertheless, it is a primary and lifelong concern, for we are identified by our sex at the moment of birth, with the cry, 'It's a boy,' or 'It's a girl,' and shortly after we are given names which will identify us by gender for life, to be followed by a comprehensive programming which will teach us what is required of us within that gender.

All this is straightforward and natural enough, and in an ideal world most of us would obligingly and comfortably take to our given gender, and other roles without qualms, and without undue sense of injury or oppression to our simple basic self.

Problems arise, however, when the developing person is confronted by demands and expectations from family and society which cannot be fulfilled without seriously distorting the integrity of the self. This can give rise to insoluble conflicts between the needs of the self and the pressures of its environment, especially when a young person is exposed to force or threats of rejection from those determined to impose rigid dogmatic standards and values.

A child under pressure to adapt in more extreme ways will resort to various coping strategies in an attempt to compromise between his or her own needs and the expectations of others. We have all had to compromise ourselves in these ways to some extent, we are all adapted people. There is always the risk that our childhood coping strategies, useful and necessary at the time, may become habitual, unconscious and neurotic, following us into adult life where they are no longer appropriate, useful, or necessary. Indeed, in an adult context, they may well be actively self-defeating.

This is why it is so important to take time out periodically, to uncover and review our old habits and patterns of relationship, so that we have a better chance of discarding, revising or replacing them.

The following sections will describe three of the commonest survival patterns we adopt to cope with stressful demands for conformity from parents, or, in later life, from our partners and society at large. These patterns are generally acknowledged to be maladaptive or neurotic in their extreme forms, yet most of us resort to them at some stage in our lives. They are offered here to help you recognise your own favourite, and perhaps unthinking and uncreative, habits of behaviour and response in relationships.

If you *do* find strong echoes of your own behaviour in the examples given below, I would encourage you to give some thought and effort to a review and reassessment of your situation. Do you have to stay as you are? Are you still using appropriate coping behaviour — or are you now coping out? Perhaps the time has come when you could safely risk letting go of old patterns of response and learn better ways of relationship, which allow you more scope to be your real self.

Projection: The Disowning Pattern

Projection is one of the better known processes by which people deal with the conflict between how they really are and how they think they should be. It generally takes the form of unconscious hypocrisy, designed to protect an unrealistically virtuous self-image by consistently finding fault with others.

Projection can operate in all forms of relationship but the opposite sex is probably the most widely and frequently used dumping ground for parts of the self we feel we must disown.

Classical projection of this kind is seen in the man who prides himself on his emotional strength, never cracks up, and has never cried since that long-forgotten time when his mother punished him for this weak unmanly behaviour. As an adult, he now perceives women in an exaggerated stereotyped way, as unreliable, weak, weepy and timorous — and quite unlike himself. By relentlessly projecting and disowning part of himself onto women, he can safely point a scornful finger at their weaknesses, while at the same time bolstering his own strong and manly image.

Or take the case of the woman whose father only showed her affection when she was being a good little girl: now she has grown into a pretty little thing, always wearing her fixed little smile, perfectly happy in her nice little job. Her only problem? Men, especially the men in her life, always turn out to be sullen, selfish, short-tempered or ruthlessly competitive. She *needs* to disown all these 'bad' traits onto the opposite sex, for these is no room for them in her limited good-girl gender image. Unconsciously, the projector maintains a superficial, black and white view of the opposite sex, by contriving to notice only what he or she expects to see.

Projection can be seen operating in its more serious forms in the alcoholic's or the compulsive gambler's wife: her life is devoted to trying to convince him that he is completely irresponsible, wasting his precious life in self-destructive addiction. It never occurs to her that she is wasting *her* life, that she might be equally addicted to her own self-sacrificing, self-denying role. Similarly, the neurotically jealous and possessive husband, who virtually locks up his wife, at least psychologically, is so obsessed with the innate promiscuity and fickleness of women, that he is able to avoid taking a closer look at his own sexual nature.

Serious degrees of projection are signalled by the high emotional charge experienced by the projector whenever he spots his favourite blemish in another. It is those faults in other people that send us into a blind fury, or make us recoil with disgust, which most need attention within ourselves. Generally speaking, when others provoke in us a burst of evangelical zeal, or a wave of self-righteous, self-congratulation, then it is time to consider what we might be projecting away from ourselves and onto 'them'.

Introjection: The Brainwashed Pattern

A questioning, open-minded attitude is essential if we are to develop our own sense of discrimination, to live according to our own real values and standards of behaviour. Unfortunately, many people grow up in situations where this ability to think and decide for themselves is either ignored or actively discouraged. A great deal of unacknowledged unconscious brain-washing goes on in the early years, when our basic ideas about gender, and other issues, are formed.

In the previous chapter the questionnaires invited you to take a long hard look at the sources of these ideas, but the details of these sexual doctrines are less important than the *way* in which you were indoctrinated. Were you force-fed, expected to swallow whole your family's values and standards of behaviour, or were you allowed to question, argue, discuss? Was your own sense of discrimination encouraged, or was it ignored or squashed out of you, on the grounds that you were only a child?

The child has no effective defence against mental force-feeding from adults who will brook no disagreement, whose own ideas are based on unquestionable family or class traditions, or backed by unchallengeable authority, for example the authority of God himself, in a religious family. To survive and remain loveable, the child will do its best to swallow whole chunks of dogma, to conform to what is required, and may grow up with no real ability to chew things over, to digest and assimilate ideas properly for him- or herself.

The psychological term for this process is 'introjection', referring to the injection of alien ideas, whole and entire, into the personality of the recipient, without critical assessment. In adult life, a person subjected to this early patterning is likely to behave either with marked timidity towards others' ideas, or assume a dogmatic stance. Both these kinds of people are essentially frightened of non-conformity, argument or disagreement, and do not value or acknowledge the individual's right to think and act at variance with the norm.

The timid introjector becomes anxious whenever he or she is asked to take a decision or make a statement of personal opinion, and the deep-rooted dread of conflict is shown in typical responses, such as, 'What do *you* think? . . . *You* decide . . . I've got no opinion either way . . . I'll do whatever *you* think is right.' Such chronic indecision and paralysis of personal judgement can often be traced back to parents who were themselves locked into insoluble conflict. Faced with battling parents, the child might internalise the entire battleground, for he or she loves both parents and wants to conform to and please both. Divided loyalties ensure that there can be no winner, and the result can only be stalemate and the immobilisation of the child's own personality.

By contrast, the dogmatic introjector is seldom, if ever, in doubt. The parents in this case probably spoke with one voice, feeding the child with their own absolute values and judgements of right and wrong. Such a person is character-ised by statements such as, 'You will, of course, agree that . . . There is a right way and a wrong way of thinking about this . . . Any reasonable person would agree that . . .' and so on. Habits of finger-wagging, a wide-eyed glare, and remorseless repetition of the facts are also typical signs of people using this pattern of relationship.

These patterns of behaviour bedevil adult relationships because there is little sense of contact with the introjector's real self: there seems to be no authentic, personal voice; only the sound of old recordings being played back in their original form, unaltered by individual experience or critical reassessment.

Retroflection: The Self-blaming Pattern

Whereas the projector will accuse others of what he dare not acknowledge in himself, the chronic self-blamer dare not express his critical or hostile thoughts about others. Instead, he turns them into an attack upon himself; in psychological terms he 'retroflects' his aggressive impulses.

As with projection, the unmanageable personality traits in question carry a high emotional charge. Typically, the self-blamer describes his faults in extreme terms. He is 'completely useless' rather than 'having difficulty with a project,' or he is 'horribly selfish and arrogant' rather than 'aware of his own needs.'

Once established, the habit of turning unwanted aggression inwards can become a vicious circle, which the sufferer constantly reinforces with a daily dose of self-denigration. This condition often underlies depression and various psycho-somatic illnesses.

For such a person, any relationship is fraught with anxiety, for any trace of disagreement or dislike on his part is felt to be taboo, and yet another sign of his permanent inner rottenness; he will therefore tend to short-circuit the tension by taking the earliest opportunity of expressing contempt or irritation *at himself*: 'I'm ashamed of myself . . . I'm angry at myself . . . I could kick myself for being so stupid.'

Once again, the origin of this self-destructive pattern can generally be traced back to coping tactics adopted in the childhood situation. Unless there is adequate allowance for the child's developing self-expression and self-assertion, the child has little choice but to hide and distort his or her own reality. The child may *feel* aggressive towards parents or siblings, and may want to point out their stupidities, injustices and hurtfulness, but if these negative feelings are punished simply for being expressed, then it may well appear that the only alternative is to feel bad about oneself. Child logic goes something like this, 'My parents must always be right, for I depend upon them and they are more powerful than I. Something feels wrong here, therefore I must be wrong,' or more succinctly, 'Anger is bad. I feel angry, therefore I must be bad.'

This position can become deeply entrenched and stoutly defended, despite its drawbacks: the self-blamer is usually highly disconcerted when asked to name just one other person in the whole world who is 'worse' than himself, for his whole image depends upon everyone else being better in some way.

He will go to almost any lengths to avoid openly confronting others in a critical way. Such a person could accurately be described as aggro-phobic, for there is a deep, irrational fear that if his negative feelings were to be expressed outwardly, even in the mildest degree, the result would be catastrophic in some unimaginable way. Whereas, in reality, it could be the first step towards developing a more robust and inter-active personality and style of relationship.

Assimilation: The Pattern Breaker

When you know *how* you habitually relate to others, and you know *which* of your patterns are no longer relevant in adult relationships, then you are in a position to take fuller charge of your own life, to look for a new pattern that will foster your development rather than hinder it.

Habits of response are largely acquired in childhood: new habits of response can be acquired in adulthood. To understand and accept this fully is a key to mobilising your ability to make positive changes now. So let me once more underline and summarise the essential difference between the two states.

Child logic is just as sound as adult logic, but the circumstances and relative power of self-determination are quite different. In childhood, especially in the early years, total dependency on others for survival is the rule, and the child-self has little choice but to adapt and conform. He or she is simply not in a position to argue, to assert, or to negotiate with others, if these activities are forbidden, and therefore *has* to resort to various coping patterns, such as we have been examining in this chapter.

The adult, however, needs above all to recognise that the *rules have changed*. The adult-self is in a different context, and needs to explore and lay claim to the full autonomy and self-determination which is now available for the taking.

It is often the case, though, that grown men and women continue to act as if the rules of childhood — obey, conform, survive — still applied. It is especially difficult to break free of childhood patterns when they were imposed through fear — of punishment or rejection — and the pressure of these old fears, keeping us confined within our old patterns, needs to be frankly acknowledged.

The work of breaking up, and breaking out of old patterns begins with a questioning attitude. How often do you question the assumptions you make in your relationships? How often do you confront and argue with the assumptions made about you in relationships? The ability and the readiness of the adult to ask 'why?' and 'why not?' is one significant indicator of his or her capacity to explore and grow within relationships. Do you allow yourself space to think things over, to assess, test and modify ideas before you take them into yourself? 'I need to think about that,' or, 'tell me more before I decide whether I agree,' are statements of self-authority.

Ideas, about gender as well as other roles, are a form of psychological food, which can nourish and develop our personalities, or stunt them and make us ill. The successful assimilation of ideas, whether they come from the past, the present or the future, depends on the condition of our psychological digestive system. The vigour with which we are prepared to ask awkward questions, to disagree, and to exercise our free choice to accept, reject or modify the multitude of ideas about gender roles which are now available in our society, is a measure of our determination to keep on growing.

Instead of projecting your problems onto others, letting others brainwash you, or kicking yourself for not being perfect, you can learn how to re-examine your current reality and resources, discover your own needs and aspirations, and begin to respond to others as an autonomous adult, rather than reacting *as if* you were still a powerless child.

The work of establishing this adult stance may take many years, for we all start out from positions of complete *dependence*, and may acquire patterns of coping which handicap our subsequent struggles towards *independence*; until we acquire a degree of autonomy, self-support and self-direction, it will be difficult to sustain adult relationships of *interdependence*. Without a stable and lively sense of self-responsible individuality, we may seek refuge in regressive mergers with our partners ('Let's stay as we are, forever!'), or continue to act out the insoluble power struggles of earlier years.

PART FOUR

TRANS-
FORMATION

CHAPTER 15

THE CHANCES OF CHANGE

BECOMING MORE YOURSELF: Do It for Me — Hey Presto!
— At the Crossroads — Steps Towards Change

BECOMING MORE YOURSELF

Your work with the Dream Lover will constantly reflect the
ways in which your own personality patterns and assumptions can frustrate and limit your relationship with yourself
and with others. Having worked your way through the
various exercises in this book, you will by now have a
clearer idea of the old ways that you would like to change,
and new ways that you would want to grow into. But how is
this to be achieved?

'How can I change?' is probably the commonest question I
am asked as a therapist. Typically, there is great urgency in
the question. The client is saying, in effect, 'I hate being like
this and I want to be different *now*!' So my first response will
be, 'Slow down, take it easy, give yourself time.'

Change, even when it is clearly beneficial and highly
motivated, is stressful. The more radical, frequent and
speedy the change, the more stress you will accumulate.
Trying your hardest for the speediest result is often simply
self-defeating. If you have ever been involved in crash diets,
instant cures, get-rich-quick schemes or whirlwind ro-
mances, you will know that this is true.

Paradoxically, for many people the first thing they need to

change is their own attitude to change, so take some time now to consider how you believe a personality change takes place. Here are just three models of such attitudes. You may identify with one of these, or you may realise that your own beliefs are somewhat different.

Do It for Me

The idea here is that one's personality problem is the same as, say, a boil between the shoulder blades. You cannot reach it yourself, it is urgent and painful, and so, naturally, you must rush from person to person demanding, 'Quick, make me better. Do it for me!'

The underlying assumption is that others have expertise or skills that you do not possess and cannot develop for yourself. This common medical analogy is deceptive because it falsely equates the personality with the body. You can take your physical symptoms to a doctor and, hopefully, have them taken away from you, and by analogy you come to believe that there will be a personality doctor who will be able to do the same sort of thing by removing your troublesome personality traits. Or perhaps you have an inner belief that eventually you will find the right partner, someone else who miraculously knows how to do the trick that at last enables you to live your own life differently.

Hey Presto!

'I've suddenly discovered that . . .' This is the preamble of the person who believes in the magic wand approach to self-change. Such a person usually goes on to say, with intense earnestness and conviction, 'And ever since that moment I've been a changed person.' Three weeks later, he or she does not want to talk about the Hey Presto moment any more. The sudden change has not taken root.

Variations of the Hey Presto concept could be called 'Mind over Matter' or 'Sheer Will Power' where force rather than speed is believed to be the magic ingredient that produces desirable change.

The point is that both 'Do it for me' and 'Hey Presto' people hope for speedy once-and-for-all transformations, whether these are expected from outside or inside that person. I doubt whether there are any short cuts that will allow us to totally by-pass the natural process of change, which is generally difficult, slow and circuitous.

So let us now consider a third model of change, one that, to me at least, looks more promising.

At the Crossroads

The crossroads symbolises a situation of choice, an opportunity to change direction, to move towards a different objective. *Or* to continue along the same path. *Or* to go back the way we came. *Or* to sit down and stay exactly where we are.

Psychologically speaking we are always surrounded by choices: we take the crossroads with us every step of the way, throughout our lives.

At the crossroads, some may delay, paralysed by fear of taking a wrong step. Others may wait for a companion to share the decision, or a guide that they can follow.

But at least, if you adopt this analogy as your model of the process of change, you will be aware that there *are* always options of behaviour; that you *can* always take an initiative and alter your direction; that there *is* a certain distance between you and your goal, and that the journey *will* take time. The crucial advantage of the crossroads symbol is that it constantly reminds us that we are personally in charge of where we go next, and how far and how fast we choose to travel.

Steps Towards Change

The natural process of change seems to follow a series of steps which take us through five major stages or 'crossroads'; these are outlined below, together with some of the difficulties you may encounter, and which may prompt you to stay put or go back at any stage.

1 Willingness to Look We need some motivation to start to look at ourselves more closely. Common reasons for taking time out to re-examine our thoughts and feelings, needs and options, include: a crisis — divorce, separation, bereavement; dissatisfaction — a sense of boredom, depression, claustrophobia in a relationship; curiosity — we want to know what other possibilities might be interesting and enjoyable in a relationship.

You may get over the crisis in time, as things return to normal. You may become resigned to your dissatisfactions, or you may change partners in order to avoid the uncomfortable job of looking for the deeper roots of your unhappiness. These are the kinds of ways we decline life's opportunities to go beyond the first step of change.

What were your own motivations for beginning to explore your relationships through dreamwork? The decision you made to work your way through this book brought you to the second stage of change:

2 Increasing Awareness Whatever brought you to dreamwork could equally have prompted you to join one of the increasing number of growth, development and awareness-raising groups throughout the country; or to seek individual counselling help in exploring your relationships; or to study psychology through reading or through an educational establishment.

All these are means of fostering the second stage of change, during which we explore our thoughts, feelings, expectations and memories, around issues of central importance in our lives.

Some of what we discover along the way may seem distasteful, frightening, frustrating. For this reason it is important to suspend judgement over what we learn. We need to silence, as best we can, the sometimes harsh and over-critical 'parents in the head', whose disapproval may cut short our self-exploration and experiments on the grounds that it is wrong or dangerous or pointless. It is therefore important that, if you do seek support in the process of exploration, whether from a group or an individual counsellor, you choose people who are non-judgemental, non-dogmatic and unprejudiced, who will give you the necessary support and encouragement to explore as widely and as deeply as you need to.

3 Acknowledging the way we are We may strongly resist 'owning up' to parts of ourselves that do not fit our ideal self-image. The difficulty of acknowledging what we find as we explore ourselves and our relationships lies in our fear that by admitting our faults we admit that we are bad, unacceptable, second-rate people.

When, as adults, we find ourselves resisting and denying that we do such and such, or that we hate so and so, we are re-living echoes from childhood. Unconsciously, we still expect to be judged, criticised or punished for our genuine difficulties in adjusting our natural selves to the expectations of our family and our culture. The way we actually are is covered with layers of ancient guilt and fear, for as children we strive to be good, to adapt and conform to the ideal that the adult world seems to require, in order that 'they' will go on loving us. So we do our best to reject our bad bits, and live out only the Good Boy or Good Girl role.

This is why the acknowledgement stage of change is perhaps the most difficult to go through. It may well seem crazy to threaten our self-esteem by stirring up the mud of past problems. Yet a basic feeling of self-worth need not be lost; it is merely somewhat disorganised for a time, and will re-form later into a more authentic and broader representation of who you really are.

To pass through this particular crossroads you may need a kind of personal banner or affirmation to remind yourself what this is all about. Perhaps something like, 'I am a good person, re-discovering some needs and prejudices I had forgotten. These problems limit my change and growth, and I am seeking ways to be more fully myself.'

4 Acceptance If we can suspend our judgements and self-criticisms for a while, we can start to be interested in, rather than rejective of, our 'bad bits', our problem areas. Our interest then allows us to examine and discuss the problem, with our partners, with our friends and with ourselves through self-reflection and research.

The exercises and self-questions presented in Part Two are all tools to encourage you in this process of dialogue between your conscious, everyday self, and other, alienated parts of you, represented in dreams of your opposite — the Dream Lover.

With dialogue comes understanding. You may come to understand that you carry within you alternative points of view on what is possible, how you could be more fulfilled in your life and in your relationships.

Dialogue and discussion will help to counter your fear of the problem. By becoming more familiar with it, you begin to reclaim the power it holds over you. Whatever unvoiced needs or fears lie behind your particular problem with the opposite sex, it is better to have these monsters out in the open, where you can see them clearly, than to pretend they don't exist and hope they will go away.

Familiarity, and perhaps in time even affection, for the problematic aspects of yourself may finally stir you into compassion for yourself; with compassion, you will be able to tolerate more of yourself. Self-acceptance means acceptance *now*, in your unfinished state, still in a process of becoming better but far short of perfection. If you wait until you are perfect before allowing yourself approval and esteem, you will spend your whole life in self-critical dissatisfaction. But if you can feel 'good enough for now', you will start to notice that people all around you are also 'good enough for now', which is bound to enhance your relationships.

148

5 Staying conscious of the problem It is not easy to stay conscious of the sort of problems we may find are undermining our relationships, such as patterns of greed, dependency, fear of sexual intimacy, resentment, etc. When we find such skeletons in our unconscious cupboards, our usual reaction may be to stuff them back out of sight again, and quickly.

It is not just problems that we want to be rid of that we relegate from awareness. For some it is equally difficult to stay aware of positive, sought-after developments, in our ideals, our virtues, our creativity. However, there is obviously little point in creating any agenda for change in yourself if you then promptly lose it again in your 'forget it' file.

Constant awareness of what we are, and what we want to be is the key to change. If we remain self-aware we *notice* what we are doing, how we do it, what we feel about it. In the process, we *notice* opportunities to do it differently, to choose to be different with this or that person. And we can choose to be different more and more frequently, until the desired change takes root and becomes a familiar part of ourselves. This is the crossroads of choice which always comes with us; to grow and change from this point on is a question of staying aware.

This book is intended to take you to this fifth crossroad, by encouraging you to explore, acknowledge and accept more of yourself, to evolve an agenda for change, and to stay aware of your goals. Any further journey is entirely up to you. I say this because I firmly believe that no one can be forced, cajoled or tricked into change from outside. The pressure for change is always, ultimately, an inner urge, an inner consent to moving on, to growth.

In the following three chapters I will discuss how this inner urge sometimes sends us signals and symbols, through our dreams, that the time is ripe for further growth and change.

CHAPTER 16

THE DREAM LOVER AS ALLY

*INVITING MORE HELPFUL DREAMS: Answers from the
Unconscious — Programming a Dream — The Ally in Action
— Case Histories*

INVITING MORE HELPFUL DREAMS

Whenever we find ourselves stuck at a crossroads of
change, unable to work out what to do or where to go next,
it is only natural that we would wish for a wise companion,
an ally whom we could consult for some sound advice and
fresh insights about our situation.

The Dream Lover is the ideal candidate for this role. Since
he or she represents the inner 'other half', which in most
cases is largely unacknowledged and undeveloped, the
Dream Lover is certainly a promising source of new ideas
and a fresh point of view in dealing with relationship problems. The only snag is that we don't seem to be able to count
on the right dream turning up at the time we need it. In this
chapter, therefore, we will explore the possibilities of evok-
ing the Dream Lover as an ally whenever we need special
help with a current relationship problem.

It may seem to you at the moment that your dreams set
their own agenda, that you have no conscious influence on
the type and content of any given dream you might have,

and that the Dream Lover leads a life of its own, appearing capriciously in its endlessly varied forms without reference to the dreamer's own priorities and preferences.

Yet most people who pay serious attention to their dream-lives find that their conscious everyday preoccupations frequently result in a dream that in some way mirrors, amplifies or even answers the unvoiced questions they may have in mind before sleep. You may yourself have noticed this two-way process between dreaming and waking concerns in your dreamwork so far — times when a row with your partner has spilled over into an angry confrontation with the Dream Lover in your sleep, or when a romantic daydream about an interesting new acquaintance leads into an even more romantic night dream.

These effects arise from the fact that the borderline between the sleeping and waking self is not so clearly drawn and rigid as we may think. The ninety-minute dreaming cycle which goes on throughout the night is the result of an alternating rhythm of deep, dreamless sleep followed by a period of lighter sleep, and it is during these lighter phases of sleep that we dream. It seems that this rhythmic rise and fall in consciousness also follows us into the day, for we all experience alternating periods of alertness and drowsiness as we go about our waking lives.

You may be more or less aware of such a pattern in your own life, — times of day when you feel wide awake, energetic and ready for anything, and other times when you feel half-asleep and find it difficult to concentrate fully. You might describe yourself as a 'morning' or an 'afternoon' person, or a 'night owl', in reference to this personal pattern of cyclic consciousness.

As we approach a low point in the day, concentration blurs and we are prone to fall into a reverie, to become preoccupied with some inner concern, to daydream. We have already made some use of these phenomena in our work with daydreams in Chapter 8. It is at such times, in our more dreamy moods, that part of our attention can float over the borderline between conscious and unconscious, and form a two-way opening between the inner and outer worlds. It is also at such times that the unconscious is more open to our conscious suggestions.

The most useful period of borderline consciousness, from a dreamwork point of view, is the time just before we drop off to sleep at night. The last few minutes of drowsy relaxation which are the prelude to sleep give us opportunities to suggest a specific purpose, or to put a specific question, to the Dream Lover waiting in the wings. This will increase our chances of having helpful dreams that night, related directly or indirectly to the problems we had in mind.

Answers from the Unconscious

There are many classic stories on record to support the validity of this two-way, question and answer process between the conscious and unconscious parts of the mind. The scientist Kekulé, after long and fruitless investigations into the atomic structure of benzene, was rewarded with a dream in which a snake seized hold of its own tail to form a circle. This bizarre symbol was enough of a creative nudge to make him realise that the benzene molecule must, after all, have a ring structure.

Among writers who have acknowledged the creative problem-solving potential of dreams are the author of the Frankenstein story, Mary Shelley, and Robert Louis Stevenson, who referred to his team of 'brownies' working behind the scenes to produce dream stories while he slept, for him to write up during the day.

We are not concerned here with scientific research or novel writing, but it is clear that there is a creative resource in our dreams which is capable, under the right conditions, of revealing fresh insights and ideas which we may not be able to come up with through our conscious efforts. Our work is focused on the Dream Lover and our relationships with the opposite sex, so let us now look at methods we could employ to encourage our unconscious to work for us in this area, by sending us dreams of the Dream Lover in the role of a helpful ally.

Programming a Dream

Problem-solving dreams occur most readily when the person concerned has spent some time and effort in preparing the ground, and is ready to receive the answer.

Characteristically, such dreams arise in response to a person's *intense absorption* with a *particular problem*, and following *concentrated efforts* to come up with a solution. The dreamer must be *highly motivated* towards change, and be *open-minded* enough to at least consider *any new approach* to the problem.

In working your way through this book so far, you are likely to have fulfilled most of the necessary pre-conditions I have just mentioned — absorption in the subject, increasing awareness of the particular problems and patterns in your life, the concentrated effort needed to practise the exercises, and an open-minded exploratory approach to change.

The only other preparatory work you need to do before trying out this technique for yourself, is to select a key issue or situation on which to focus your attention. You are proposing to ask your Dream Lover for help and advice, and the clearer the question, the clearer will be the answer: you need to know what it is that you need to know!

You may already have your own key question in mind: 'Where can I meet a different kind of man?', 'How will I ever get over Miss X?', 'How can I stop being so self-sacrificing?', 'What do I need most from my relationships now?', and so on. Generally speaking, the more urgent and painful the situation, the more frustrated and stuck you feel around a particular issue, the higher will be the emotional pressure on your unconscious other half to come up with a significant response.

If, on the other hand, you can't readily formulate your

key question, it will help to look back through your dream diary and review the results of any exercises you have worked with. Look particularly for themes, repetitious situations and scenarios that have left you feeling dissatisfied or puzzled. Then review your current or recent relationships with a view to uncovering any theme or pattern here that is problematical for you. Ask yourself, 'Where am I stuck . . . what am I repeating . . . what do I do that is self-defeating . . . what traps me . . . what frightens or angers me . . . what is most urgent? If there was *one thing* I could change in the way I relate to the opposite sex, what would it be?'

Having selected the issue and the key question that is most important for you at this time, you are ready to invite the Dream Lover to cooperate by inspiring a dream that will give you a fresh insight into your problem.

To do this, I suggest that you spend a short time during the evening (fifteen minutes is enough) thinking over the problem, reviewing the pros and cons and the particular difficulties you are having in coming to a solution. Then forget it until bedtime. Finally, just before you go to sleep, remind yourself that your Dream Lover is now a willing ally, who will take care of your problem while you sleep. Ask your question in this frame of mind, and then relax and let go of the subject altogether.

When you wake, take special care to record any dream you remember as fully as possible, regardless of its seeming relevance to your problem; you will be able to decide later, after further work on the dream, whether or not it is useful to you.

The Ally in Action

The following two case studies include important dreams obtained in this way. By asking for, and being open to advice and insight from the Dream Lover, both these people were helped to find new directions out of relationship

154

situations that had previously seemed thoroughly stuck.

In both cases, the key dream contains a direct reference to the actual person on whom the dreamer's current problem is focused. This made it easier to accept the connection between the dream content and the problem. However, the connection is not always so plain, and you should be prepared to explore *any* form of dream that comes to you after you have used this technique, *as if* it were a direct answer to your problem.

Case history 1   Rosemary was in her late twenties and making good progress in her chosen career. Her two-year marriage to Thomas provided a mutually supportive and satisfying partnership for two ambitious people who, at this stage in their lives, were focused on developing their careers.

A deepening shadow was being cast over the relationship as Rosemary discovered that she could not rely on Thomas to respond sympathetically to her occasional bouts of distress and worry about her work. On one occasion he had left abruptly for the pub when she tried to talk about her fears and self-doubts after a reorganisation in the office had resulted in staff redundancies.

'He seems to be warning me off all the time,' she complained. 'It seems it's taboo for me to bring any bad feelings of uncertainty and neediness to him. He says I'm becoming neurotic, I should learn to stand on my own feet more, and not moan about my problems.

'What really undermines me, though, is that I half agree with him in this. I've always tried to be very independent, and I ask myself why *should* I burden him with my troubles — I should be able to take care of myself. But I can't stand these awkward scenes. I do need to talk it over with him sometimes, yet I feel guilty when he obviously can't handle it.'

Rosemary began to find herself matching Thomas's unpredictable withdrawals of emotional support by withdrawing herself, and keeping her difficulties from him, but what she described as a 'war going on inside my head' continued. 'I'm being pulled two ways all the time. I need to feel independent and strong, but independence and self-sufficiency are not so great when I'm feeling weak and weepy.'

In essence, Rosemary's problem was to find a new way to get beyond this impasse of uncertainty, and her key question came down to this. 'Where is the root cause of my inner conflict about independence?'

Within a week, this simple focusing phrase resulted in the following dream. Like many dreams, it was remembered as a series of separate little episodes. Such dreams are often recorded as separate unconnected stories but since they occur in one dreaming sequence it is more fruitful to consider them together, as a series of 'comments' linked to a central topic.

My husband is leading me down some concrete steps into the basement of some sort of industrial building or laboratory. It is very cold, but brightly lit and clean. I understand that we are going down here to meet his mother. We are paying her one of our 'dutiful visits'. But we can't find her. My husband leads the way through a series of corridors, opening doors, calling for her. It's a huge place, full of white rooms, bright, cold and empty. It's like a cold store — as we open each door, a gust of frosty air comes out.

In the next dream, we are in our living room at home, having an intense argument. It's extremely frustrating for me, because all he does is repeat back what I say to him. He's standing facing me, copying me. When I put my hands on my hips, he puts *his* hands on his hips. When I shake my head, he shakes his head. When I shout. 'Stop fooling around and listen to me,' he says the same, like an echo. I just can't get my point across to him — and I can't now remember what I was trying to say anyway. The main point was the frustration of his mocking and mimicking me.

In the last dream I was again with a man, an anonymous figure, shadowy: I suppose it could have been my husband, but I couldn't identify him now, and it wasn't important at the time. There we were, back in the basement, but now it was dark and spooky. I felt frightened. Suddenly, he shouted and pointed, 'Look out, behind you!' I was really scared. I looked around but could see nothing in the corridor. I ran to the corner to look down a side corridor — nothing. I felt very uneasy, as if someone was creeping up behind me whichever way I turned, but I could never catch sight of anyone.

In this remarkable series of dreamlets, Rosemary's Dream Lover directs her attention first to Thomas's absent mother, then gives a broad hint that Rosemary's conflicts are mirrored in her relationship with her partner, and finally points out that she is herself being haunted by someone behind her, in her past.

This becomes clearer if we remind ourselves of Rosemary's question ('Where is the root cause of my inner conflict about independence?') We can then see that the Dream Lover is responding by saying, 'Look at the significance of Thomas's relationship with his mother, then consider the similarities between you, and then realise that you are scared of some part of your life that you have put out of sight, behind you.'

From what she knew of Thomas's background, Rosemary could readily acknowledge the first dream as an accurate reflection on his mother, whom he pictured as cold and absent, often too busy to give him the amount of attention he felt he needed. As a child, Thomas had learned to withdraw from his uncomfortable feelings of hurt, rejection and loneliness, and also learned to mimic some of his mother's own rather stern mottoes about self-sufficiency — the virtues of standing on one's own feet at an early age, the dangers of spoiling a child with too much attention, and so on. Now, as an adult, Thomas often responded to Rosemary in the same way that his mother had responded to *his* anxious feelings, by giving her lectures about grown-up behaviour, and by refusing to indulge her with too much sympathy.

Already, these reflections were giving Rosemary fresh insights into more fruitful ways of discussing her difficulties with Thomas, but the second and third dream scenes took her much further than this, by pointing out that the couple share similar difficulties. Perhaps, then, the root cause of Rosemary's own admitted conflicts about independence also arose from early difficulties between mother and child? Perhaps indeed, the unknown, unseen figure that was giving her so much anxiety in the third part of the dream was her own mother.

It was this latter realisation that proved to be a key to Rosemary's subsequent self-development work, unlocking much unfinished business that was still deeply troubling her and affecting her relationship.

It is not appropriate here to give more than a brief indication of the issues involved in Rosemary's relationship with her mother but the following notes illustrate how even the most highly charged unresolved emotional situations can be put 'out of sight, out of mind', until we feel strong enough to deal with them more safely, at a later date.

Rosemary was a late and only child, whose parents had divorced when she was six years old. As a lone parent, her mother had thereafter played an exaggerated and crucial role in her development, by her well-intentioned but over-done devotion to her daughter's life. In fact, Rosemary grew up dominated by her mother's anxious, over-protective and ultimately possessive obsession with her welfare. In her teens and early twenties she had been forced to assert her own growing independence more and more frequently and fiercely, in order to survive as a separate person.

'When I suffered, she suffered with me, only more so!' she recalled. 'I could hardly have a day off work with a cold without her worrying and phoning and making it into a crisis on my behalf. I learned to hide what was going on for me. I had to keep even minor troubles to myself because I couldn't bear the way she invaded me and tried to live my life for me.'

This distressing situation had been further compounded by the mother's death, a year before Rosemary's marriage. She was thus carrying a considerable burden of unresolved grief, guilt, anger, and fear of being controlled by close relationships, all of which she managed to keep more or less to herself, as was her habit, within the marriage. Ironically, she had chosen a partner who also believed that the safest way of dealing with distress was to keep quiet about it but for quite opposite reasons, and it was this aspect of the situation that we can see mirrored with uncanny accuracy in the second part of Rosemary's dream.

Case history 2   In contrast to Rosemary, the focal point of Colin's problem was all too obvious. At the age of fifty-one he had, for the first time in his twenty-five-year marriage, fallen in love and had a short affair with a much younger woman, Sylvia. His wife had quickly discovered the infidelity and had reacted with shock and intense jealousy.

This couple had enjoyed a long and satisfactory marriage, and there was no real threat of a break-up, for religious reasons as well as the fact that there were three children still in their teens and living at home. But despite the reality that the affair had been over and done with for two years, the emotional aftermath was still proving a great strain for both partners.

Colin was just as disturbed by his own infatuation and untypical behaviour as was his wife. He still felt guilty and depressed, and lived with the unsettling idea that if it had happened once, it could easily happen again. His wife made it clear that she no longer trusted him, and suspiciously monitored his life, making jealous comments whenever he had even the most casual social contact with other women. To make matters worse, Colin and his ex-lover both worked in the same office block and occasional chance encounters were inevitable. On such occasions, he felt he had no control over his reaction: the very sight of her pitched him straight back into an emotional whirlpool of guilt, longing, and ungovernable fantasies.

On a rational level, Colin could acknowledge that he was being plagued by an infatuation with his own inner fantasies. In reality, Sylvia could never have lived up to the awesomely powerful image of youth, beauty and innocent idealised love that he was projecting onto her. Perhaps his wife, too, intuitively understood that her rival was now more in his head than in outer reality. Yet the continuing stress for both partners was no less real for all that. Colin, in fact, confessed that he privately feared his crazy emotionality was the prelude to a nervous breakdown.

This idea was reinforced by a series of worrying physical symptoms including palpitations, insomnia, fatigue and severe cramps in his legs and back, all typical signs of someone under high stress.

Clearly, Colin needed all the reassurance and support he could get, not only from our counselling relationship and from sympathetic friends, but also from within, from his own psychic resources. He was very clear about what he wanted: his question to the Dream Lover was to be, 'What will heal me of this obsession?', and there was no doubt that he was highly motivated in seeking help from a dream.

In fact, Colin had several important dreams during this period, but the one I have recorded here proved to be the key dream for him:

> I am visiting Bolivia. I am talking to a middle-aged man at his desk, in the foyer of an office building. We are agreeing that 'the early bird catches the worm', that by starting work at 6 a.m. one is bound to succeed, being three hours ahead of everyone else.
>
> A woman enters. It's Sylvia. I feel the familiar surge of mixed feelings, guilt, longing, dread. She fails to recognise me, perhaps because we have met by chance in South America. I thankfully go along with this. We will act as if we didn't know each other, but I still feel slightly anxious that she will recognise me.
>
> She has brought some herbal prescriptions which will help to heal me. The prescriptions are written on white paper flowers cut from pieces of wallpaper. Another man at the desk, in a white coat, translates these onto little coloured cards, which I can take to a herbalist and obtain the right herbs. Looking at the cards, I hear the woman saying what they are for, mentioning two or three sets of symptoms. One, I remember, is for 'nervous heart'. One herb I remember was 'May'.

> I am very pleased and thankful for this service. She, I understand, is in Bolivia on a religious pilgrimage. There is some confusion and embarrassment about whether we will meet again. I am relieved to hear that she will leave tomorrow.

In this chapter, we have been considering the Dream Lover in its helpful role, as an inner ally. In this dream it steps forward in an even more direct and positive role, and we see the Dream Lover as the inner healer, for this was undoubtedly a healing experience for Colin.

Colin's story is a classic example of one of the major themes which can emerge for both men and women during the mid-life transition: the poignant and sometimes desperate struggle to regain, from outside ourselves, the experience of youth which we think is fading within ourselves. It is hard to imagine what else a beautiful young woman could symbolise for a middle-aged man, if not his own longing for the youth he feels he is losing. It is difficult to see what else could heal his distress, if not a reassurance from within that he still carries 'spring' in his own soul. With an astonishing and moving simplicity, this short dream accomplishes this purpose for him.

He finds himself in a strange country, an unknown continent (part of his own unconscious) where he would naturally expect unusual new experiences. He is talking to himself (the other middle-aged man in the foyer) on the subject of wakening at dawn, and enjoying the energy at the beginning of a new day.

Sylvia appears but acts as if she were not the real Sylvia. The relationship is ambivalent, there is uncertainty about their identities, and Colin's usual anxious reaction is held in check. He can thus experience her in a radically different role: not the longed-for object of his impossible desires but as the healer, offering him the symbols that he is to take into himself (the herbal medicines) and integrate, in order to cure his distress. The key symbol is the white flower of the May tree, the herald of spring and early summer.

The reference to her 'religious pilgrimage' further underlines the message that this transaction is on a different psychic level, set apart from their former relationship.

This is a dream which more or less speaks for itself in the context of the dreamer's life situation. However, I would like to offer a few more words of explanation about the connection between Colin's stress symptoms and the herbal prescriptions in the dream. Where did these prescriptions come from? And should Colin have followed the Dream Lover's advice and started taking infusions of May flowers?

Some years before, he had had a passing interest in herbalism, and had bought one or two popular books on the subject. The dream prompted him (and me) to look up the properties of May, which is usually listed as Hawthorn, in a herbal reference book. There we found confirmation of its usefulness in treating, among other things, insomnia, cramps, and various conditions of the heart.

Now, whilst this information is a gratifying confirmation of the retentive powers of the unconscious — it is said that we never forget anything we have heard, read or experienced in life — it would be utterly foolish to take instructions and advice *uncritically* from our dreams. The fact that we can obtain insights and a different perspective from our deeper inner resources does *not* mean that we can safely abandon our rational and practical faculties. The final stage of any dreamwork is to check it out against the yardstick of everyday waking reality. Had he wished, Colin could have consulted a qualified herbalist for advice and treatment but in the event the experience of the dream itself worked its healing process in him, and the symptoms began to abate.

This raises a further question: 'Can we heal ourselves?' to which the short answer is, 'Yes'. But if the question is, 'Can we *always* heal ourselves, of *anything*?' the answer I must give is, 'I don't know, but perhaps we can do more than we think.'

In the case we have been considering, I don't really know how or why this dream proved to be a turning point, a beginning of healing for Colin. I do know, however, from personal experience, and from sharing the experience of others, that we sometimes have such a good dream that the experience of the dream itself has a definite and positive healing effect on us psychically, and we awaken feeling that an issue, a problem, or an illness has somehow been re-solved.

In this area, we can never hope to 'know it all'. The human psyche simply doesn't conform to our current limits of understanding, our 'whys' and 'hows'; it is always more than we think. Yet, looking again at this dream, I now see that there may be a clue in the last line, where Colin dreams, 'I am relieved to hear that she will leave tomorrow', i.e. he will begin to feel better. Better *because* the symbolic figure that has possessed and preoccupied him for two years will now leave him in peace, having fulfilled its healing func-tion.

'Sylvia the Healer' was only one temporary aspect of Colin's Dream Lover. Perhaps he will use her image again, in future dreams, perhaps not. A multitude of alternative forms is always available to the Dream Lover. What is significant is that he was able to transform a negative image of the opposite sex ('Sylvia the Obsession') into a positive one.

She started out as the problem and turned into the sol-ution.

Actually, all that changed was the dreamer's attitude. The Dream Lover, the opposite sex, can be regarded as the opposition, the competition, and, in extreme cases, the enemy. Or it can be seen as complementary, cooperative, a creative source, our ally. In either case, we will tend to get just what we expect, but if we remember that the Dream Lover *belongs to us*, whatever its form, then it clearly makes more sense to approach it with a positive expectation of cooperative partnership, than to continue in unconscious unthinking conflict.

An attitude of entrenched opposition and conflict towards part of ourselves is just as distressing and destructive as an attitude of conflict towards others. When we decide to transform the Dream Lover from adversary to ally, we initiate a basic and far-reaching change in our attitudes. We not only engage the assistance of a dynamic part of our own inner selves, releasing its creative potential for development, we are also calling a truce in the so-called sex war, and softening up some of the fixed attitudes and gender boundaries which can seriously hamper our external relationships.

CHAPTER 17

DREAM CHILDREN

SYMBOLS OF CHANGE AND DEVELOPMENT: Symbolic Dream Births — The Child Archetype

SYMBOLS OF CHANGE AND DEVELOPMENT

A relationship with the Dream Lover is a dynamic and life-long affair, and a constant source of inner change and development. It is not surprising, therefore, that the fruits of this relationship appear from time to time in the form of Dream Children.

Men, as well as women, can have the experience of giving birth to new parts of themselves in dreams. These events can occur in normal ways, and also in ways that seem quite bizarre unless they are understood symbolically.

Whatever form they take, the children of our dreams are such important indicators of the state of our inner process of change that a short detour from our main theme is necessary in this chapter, to give closer consideration to the meaning of these phenomena.

Dreams in which children appear in a natural way are common. A woman may have dreams in which she is pregnant or actually giving birth, or she may simply find herself with a child in her arms from 'nowhere'. A male dreamer, on the other hand, usually finds himself in his natural role of witnessing, or assisting the female dream figure in the various stages of pregnancy, labour and delivery, although he too may simply find himself with a baby in his arms from nowhere. Both sexes are also likely to find themselves accompanied by or meeting with older children, as opposed to babies.

Dream children may appear in the form of the dreamer's own real-life off-spring or other actual children known to the dreamer, or they may be made-up figures, created entirely from the womb of the dreamer's unconscious.

In the first case, dreams about real children can be considered in the same way as dreams about real people (see Chapter 6). Our responses to real children in dreams may reflect the whole truth, part of the truth, or no truth at all about them, but may reveal a great deal about our own expectations, anxieties and projections.

In the second case, where the dream children are not known to the dreamer, it is clearly easier to look at them in terms of what they symbolise and represent of ourselves.

Here, for example, is the dream of a woman in her thirties, suffering from depression:

> I am going somewhere by continually looking back, trying to recognise and remember the route. I have an uneasy feeling that I'll end up where I started. I'm on a road that narrows into a tunnel, because there is a concrete-block wall on the left, which slants in until it almost meets the rock wall on the right. The gap looks too small for me to pass through. Beyond is a beautiful green park in the sunlight. Two little boys come along, and I spend time telling them that *they* can go through, and that it is safe, and that there is a beautiful park beyond, for them to
> . play in.

Looking at this dream, I am struck by the wistful longing of the adult woman, who is too big now to escape from the hard confines of her grown-up responsibilities and play in the sunshine. So she unconsciously creates a double measure of child-like freedom and playfulness, in the form of the two dream children, and concentrates on reassuring and encouraging *them* to play in the park. What a difference it would make if she could begin to give herself the same support in rediscovering and exploring her own playful and spontaneous side as an adult.

To take another example, here is a dream from a man in his forties:

> I dreamed that I was watching my own mother giving birth. I had a close-up and very detailed view as the new baby emerged. It was a girl, emphatically so. Her sex was so clearly and prominently displayed that I noticed nothing else. It seemed as if the whole point of the birth was to underline and engrave on my memory this one significant fact: this is a *female* child. I felt a tremendous warmth and affection for the baby — I loved her straight away . . .

This man had been brought up somewhat starved of the company of the opposite sex. He was the youngest of four brothers, his mother was a busy professional woman whose attention was necessarily rationed among the five males in the family, and he was educated at boys-only boarding schools.

Consequently, he had a strong tendency to over-idealise, almost to worship, the women he was involved with as an adult. His fixation on his own fantasies about the gender difference was very marked, and led to constant difficulties in relationships. His self-development work centred around bridging the wide gap between his inner conviction that women were mystical unknowable creatures from some other magic world, and the reality of the actual women that he encountered in real life.

This dream, which occurred during his work on this problem, could be taken as an encouraging sign of progress. Here was emphatic evidence that his own inner feminine side was stirring into life. His dream girl-child, the psychic equivalent of the sister he never had, provided a focus for further work in coming to terms with the mysterious opposite sex element in himself, countering the distorting effects of projecting this too strongly onto others.

Symbolic Dream Births

When dream children appear in dreams by more or less normal means and in more or less normal form, most people will have little difficulty in acknowledging these as symbols of their own inner child, representing their constant potential to be renewed or to grow and change.

Where they come from, and why they appear at a particular time, are interesting questions. I take the view that dream children are more likely to appear in a person's dreams when that person is consciously working to understand more of his or herself, reaching for and relating to the unknown other half, working, for example, with the Dream Lover.

The new births that spring from this activity can sometimes occur in strange ways, and the form of the new arrival can be purely symbolic. Here are just two brief illustrations of the way this can happen: a man pulls out a troublesome tooth, which falls to the floor and turns into a brightly coloured living beetle; a woman responds to her lover's touch by giving birth to a flood of live goldfish.

Both these dreams occurred in the context of the dreamers' preoccupations with spiritual development, for both were working on that area in their lives at that time. According to Jung, the scarab beetle is a classic example of a spiritual rebirth symbol, being one of the forms taken on by the sun-god during his periodic resurrection, in ancient Egyptian myths. The flood of goldfish can be readily understood as indicating a renewal of rich spiritual life, if we remember that the fish is a central and recurrent symbol in the story of Christ, who is often referred to as 'The Fisherman', performing miracles with the loaves and fishes, and so on.

These dreamers are producing something new, something unpredictable, and something with a life of its own, from out of themselves, and this clearly is a shorthand description of the birth process, no matter how strange the offspring appear at first sight. Indeed, the impressive strangeness of such symbolic new arrivals positively invites the dreamer to apply dreamwork techniques to obtain a fuller understanding of these signals of inner change.

The point is that the central process of change, and the appearance of new things for the dreamer to develop, can take many forms. By learning to recognise the analogies of birth which occur in dreams, we are therefore more able to work on such dreams with understanding.

Generally speaking, I would consider any dream in which any part of the body 'buds off' or produces anything, especially something which seems to increase or to have a life of its own, as potentially signifying that the dreamer is giving birth to some new or underdeveloped part of the personality. The most fruitful starting point for further work on these new-born symbols is to use the association and dialogue exercises described in Chapters 5 and 7.

Here, then, is another more detailed example of this sort of dream:

> There is a beautiful temple which houses a collection of special crystals, and which is guarded and managed exclusively by an all-male priesthood. The crystals are powerful sources of healing and harmony.
>
> I am impelled by the idea that these wonderful crystals should not be kept from the people in this way. The priests are jealously guarding and withholding the crystals to maintain their own power and status, and this seems wrong to me.
>
> I disguise myself as a man and enter the temple as one of the crowd. I intend to steal some of the crystals but I know that as I leave I will be questioned and searched by the priests. So I hide the crystals inside my body — in my vagina — and manage to evade the search and escape from the temple.
>
> My plan is to distribute the crystals freely in the outside world, among people who need them. Although I have stolen only a few, there will be plenty to go round, for they can be broken up into small pieces and will somehow grow again.

This was dreamt by a woman in her thirties, who was actively involved in developing her own healing gifts. Since she was at the time particularly interested in the healing properties of certain types of crystals, their appearance in the dream was a clear reference to this aspect of her life.

Although the acute anxiety involved in stealing the crystals from the watchful priests made this a heavy and disturbing dream for her at the time, on an unconscious level she is clearly optimistic of success; the crystals are released and multiplied abundantly through her reproductive act. First she takes them into herself and then gives birth to them again, outside the temple. Although it *feels* like a dangerous act of theft, stirring up guilt and fear in herself, she is really only reclaiming or liberating something which belongs to her in the first place.

There is always conflict and competition between the orthodox and unorthodox view in any field, and so her anxieties about being judged too irrational or strange in her alternative healing work could be understood in a cultural context: odd new radical ideas are generally viewed with initial suspicion by established opinion.

There is also a more personal issue for her in this dream. Those stern, authoritarian and controlling priests are showing her one of the more forbidding faces of her own Dream Lover, part of her inner picture of the masculine. The origin of this strict, negative aspect of her inner male is another story and cannot be pursued here. However, in so far as she is able to develop the courage to go against this rigid and limiting image, she gives herself more freedom to develop, to 'give birth' to more of her self.

The Child Archetype

The Child is an archetypal human symbol, and has universal cultural and religious associations of innocence, rebirth, change, hope, the future, and so on. Among other things, it symbolises the mystery of the origin of life, ever the same, ever new.

As with all symbols, you would need to explore your own personal thoughts, feelings, attitudes and memories of children in general to achieve a full understanding of what a dream child means for you. You need to be aware of your personal context as well as the cultural context (as discussed in Chapter 2) to see clearly your relationship to your inner child.

In order to do this, I suggest that you start with a piece of paper headed 'Children', and write down all the words you can possibly think of which are associated in your mind with children in general. Such a potent symbol is bound to be extremely rich in associations, and your list of qualities is likely to be a long one.

If you are honest, you will acknowledge that children can have negative associations as well as positive ones. The average person's list may include words like: boisterous, untidy, disruptive, tantrums, vulnerable, needy, demanding, disobedient, dirty, as well as spontaneous, creative, open, fresh, innocent, charming, joyous, exciting.

This list could be a starting point for you to explore your basic reactions and responses to the Child as a symbol of change and development, and at the same time could form a broad statement of your reactions, hopes and fears when faced with an opportunity to change within yourself.

There is one further important point to consider when you find a child among your dream images: what is the apparent age of that child? The age of the child that you are dreaming of may relate to yourself at that age, and you may find it revealing and helpful to consider the whole dream in the context of what was going on in your own childhood at that time.

As I said in Chapter 15 (see p. 143), we have an inner urge towards change and growth, and dream children are one means by which we can pick up signals that the time is ripe for further development. How you respond to children — the quintessential symbol of change — will tell you much about your own willingness or difficulties in accepting and trusting your personal process of change.

Children need nurturing, protection and encouragement, but will you give similar loving care and attention to your own emergent self, your new beginnings, your efforts towards changing and developing your own potential?

CHAPTER 18

THE CHALLENGE OF THE DREAM LOVER

BECOMING YOUR OWN OPPOSITE: Role Fixation —
Becoming an Adult — Young and Single — The Parent Role —
In Mid-life — Balancing Opposites — The Next Chapter

BECOMING YOUR OWN OPPOSITE

The single most striking and intriguing fact about the Dream Lover is its rich variety of forms; the man or woman of our dreams seems to have an endless repertoire of gender-based roles, a natural ability to display to us the many-sided diversity of our other half.

In this regard, the Dream Lover functions as a custodian of our potential for development, looking after all those aspects of ourselves that we have no room for in our current conscious identity, and which we tend to hide from ourselves under the veil of the 'otherness' of the opposite sex. In our dreams, we are constantly reminded of this buried treasure within, for at each appearance the Dream Lover is saying to us, in effect, 'Here I am again, in yet another form. Remember, there is much more to your personality than you think!' This is how we are challenged from within, by our own opposite, urging us to develop and reclaim our fuller selves.

In contrast to this inner abundance, many men and women lead needlessly narrow lives, confined to their respective sides of the sexual boundary lines, because they identify too closely with the gender images, prejudices and expectations handed down by their immediate family and social setting. Once having 'learned their lines', mastered the given masculine or feminine role in early life, they are reluctant to question or modify their self-concept in any way, and project the idea that the opposite sex, too, is fixed and defined for ever.

It is this fixed position that I have been challenging throughout this book, and for two reasons. First, I believe that any such arbitrary and dogmatic division of the human personality into separate male and female categories hinders the process of our wider self-development. If we take these differences too literally, we alienate ourselves from a major part of our own inner potential, and will tend to bring with us a divisive attitude of conflict in our relationships.

Secondly, I believe that many of the gender attitudes that we learn by rote in our formative years are seriously out of step with the volatile experimental and unpredictable social context of the late twentieth century. We forget how close we are to the outdated and inappropriate gender models of Edwardian and even late Victorian times; the bridge across the generations is a very short one. A person of thirty-five today, for example, will have been brought up by parents imbued with the sexual attitudes of the grandparents, which date back to well before the First World War.

These are the main reasons why I think we should always remain wary of becoming stuck and fixed in narrow roles and limited definitions around our gender identities, and why I recommend that you keep in touch with your Dream Lover to see what else there is for you to be at every stage of your life.

Role Fixation

The main drama of opposite sex relationships — and of personal growth — is bracketed between the onset of puberty and late middle age. Along the way, there are hosts of possible roles for each gender to play.

A moment's thought will give us dozens of familiar examples of sexually-determined parts that are available within this drama: Harassed Housewife, Family Man, Mother Figure, Father Figure, Hen-pecked Husband, Devoted Spouse, Cinderella, Peter Pan, and more exotically, Monk, Vestal Virgin, Casanova, Femme Fatale, Witch, Play-Boy, Florence Nightingale, Merry Widow, Dirty Old Man, and so on. These are just a few of the multitude of aspects of the self that we may discover within us, and perhaps play at for a while. They represent potentials, which are not necessarily good or bad, unless we allow ourselves to become fixated or type-cast in a particular role, excluding all other possibilities.

In becoming a stereotype of any kind, we create problems and limitations for ourselves and for those around us, and if we conceive our sexual identities in terms of a single carica-ture image, then our relationships are likely to remain equally stunted and superficial.

In this final chapter, therefore, I want to discuss four particular life situations which are important to this subject, because they frequently become sticking points in people's lives. These situations are: adolescence, young adult-hood, parent-hood, and middle-age. Each stage has its own special stresses and dilemmas which can lead people to adopt a restricted gender role, thereby hindering the pro-cess of their further self-development.

Becoming an Adult

The transition from the pre-sexual, dependent, childhood condition, to a fully sexual status with some degree of independence, makes the adolescent phase of human devel-opment one of the most difficult and trying times we shall ever have to face. I think it is fair to say that everyone experiences the full meaning of the phrase 'identity crisis' during this period of their lives.

Ungovernable emotional swings and major changes in body size, shape and functions, combine to make us seriously doubt whether we will ever again control our lives or our identities. Indeed, the teenager is often characterised by the single word 'uncontrollable'.

In the midst of this turmoil, the crucial need is for a firm identity, a sense of being someone or something definite and credible, to fill the void that has opened up between the child and early adult states. Same-sex cliques, gangs and clubs give temporary shelter, safety in numbers, protection for the naked ego of uncertain identity. We are obsessively concerned with our style, our image, with being acceptable, or at least invisible, among our peers.

We are ultra-sensitive to criticism, whilst ourselves maintaining a defensive barrage of criticism against the grown-ups and later the authorities. We tend to define ourselves by rebelling and reacting against the established order, by taking up extreme opposite attitudes. We hope not to be found out in our uncertainties, and so affect cynical and aggressive stances to cover the emotional melt-down within.

Whilst we are in this most vulnerable state, which can last for seven or eight years, any additional stress or traumatic event — death or divorce in the family, sexual abuse, trouble at school — is liable to make us recoil from the difficulties of achieving adulthood, and make us cling to our more familiar child role. This is the time when some people make the unconscious decision never to grow up and to settle instead for the chronically dependent, emotionally immature gender roles of a Peter Pan or a Wendy, a Living Doll or a Boy Wonder.

I have met many such 'adult teenagers', including men and women in their sixties, still resisting and denying the teenage imperative to move on to adult self-responsibility, and still wistfully looking for adulthood outside themselves, in the form of a guru or leader, who will take responsibility for their lives in some way. When people become fixed in child-like roles, the process of physical and mental maturation continues normally but the development of emotional maturity has stopped, perhaps permanently, at an adolescent level.

The appearance of older wiser figures is common in young people's dreams, and the Dream Lover may appear in the guise of real-life adult models. A teenage student, dreaming of making love to her middle-aged tutor, does *not* need a sexual affair with him in reality but on a psychological level she does need to discover and join with her own developing adult identity. The essential attraction of such dream figures is their magic aura of adult identity and sophistication that is so ardently sought in adolescence. They can also carry overtones of unconscious longing for a father or mother substitute, some strong reliable and caring figure that will provide a temporary emotional support during the stress and upheaval of these transitional years.

Teenage crushes, those romantic fixations on idealised love-objects, are common motifs of both daydreams and night dreams during adolescence. Unless we learn to grow out of these fantasies, by accepting that our idols have feet of clay, they may form the basis of later unrealistic searchings for the fairy-tale Perfect Partner, (as discussed in Chapter 9).

The onset of stronger, more explicitly sexual desire after puberty, with its attendant fears and uncertainties, is also frequently mirrored in dreams. I recall the dream of an eighteen-year-old woman in which she is pushing a pram along a dark street at night, followed by the menacing figure of an unknown man. Every time she tries to cross the road to escape him, a red traffic light confronts her and she has to stop at the kerb.

The red traffic light is a complex symbol, and includes associations to: red-light district — sexual promiscuity; periodically appearing red — menstruation, fertility; red — danger, stop. The pram, too, suggests her fear of pregnancy should she not control her sexuality. But it also hints that part of her is still too much of a child to fully enter into adult sexual relations. In the dream, *her* dangerous sexuality is neatly disowned, and transformed into *his* sexuality, in the guise of the prowling man.

But he is her Dream Lover, reminding her of her own, increasingly powerful, adult sexuality; this is what she is still trying to escape from but which she actually needs to accept and integrate into her maturing personality.

Young and Single

Having forged some sort of identity of our own during the turbulent teenage years, we enter the next phase of life as unattached singles. The newly-won freedom from the worst of the soul-searching uncertainties which absorbed our energies during the transition into young adulthood, enables us to enter enthusiastically into the challenge of making our own ways in the larger world. This release from the boundaries of childhood is symbolised by the key which we traditionally receive on the twenty-first birthday.

Now we can claim our rights in the world; now we can try on some of life's grown-up uniforms, test our capacities to affect events. Now we can try out the relationships we have dreamed about, and experiment with the life-styles that interest us.

During this period, the largely theoretical ideas and attitudes we asserted so dogmatically during the teens can be tested out and tempered in the light of personal experience. This is a time of buoyant optimism and willingness to experiment in our careers, in our relationships, for we are carried along and protected by the magical high energy, enthusiasm and resilience of youth.

In relationships, the key issue now becomes the choice between independence and commitment. The very idea of settling down can be most unattractive during the euphoric early years of the twenties, for there is too much to do, too much to explore, too many new people to meet. During this phase, we start off learning how to make and break relation-ships, and may have a series of more or less superficial try-outs with the opposite sex. But as the years go by, the next developmental challenge begins to engage our atten- tions: are we yet ready or able to enter into deepening intimacy, with one long-term partner, or will we defer or avoid this possibility?

At this point, unconscious expectations about marriage become important, and, of course, the main picture from which our attitudes to commitment arise will be the models of our own parents' relationships. Depending on whether this was good, bad or indifferent, we will have correspond-ing gut feelings as we consider our own prospects in long-term committed relationships.

The main work involved in establishing a creative re-warding interdependent relationship on our own terms, is contained in Part Two of this book, 'Exploration' (see p. 37). Here, many of the key issues and difficulties of deepening intimacy are discussed, with constant reference to the im-ages of the Dream Lover as an inner guide. This work largely concerns our own willingness and efforts towards increasing self-awareness and development, and is mir-rored in the success or failure of our relationships. This is a process which cannot, in my view, be avoided, if we wish to enhance and deepen our personal identities and our rela-tionships.

Again, as in our teens, we have the choice of avoiding the issue altogether; again, we can decide to remain as we are, refusing to develop our gender identities any further than the 'young and single' phase. In doing so, we risk becoming locked into another set of gender stereotypes — the Eternal Butterfly, flitting from one superficial relationship to the next; the Playboy, always cashing in his chips before the game has really begun; Casanova, collecting his worthless trophies of conquest.

These are some of the 'stuck' gender roles we might adopt to avoid the hard work of further development, but they are all roles that become increasingly difficult to maintain, as life goes on and we become jaded, dissatisfied and, ultimately, lonely, within our round of shallow and temporary liaisons. In trying to avoid the 'trap' of deeper intimacy, we can become trapped in the compulsive anxieties of constant avoiding action.

The main part of this book is devoted to dealing with the problems of closer relationships, so I will close this section by mentioning only one futher Dream Lover image, chosen because it typifies the anxieties that might face the young and single, as they contemplate moving on into deeper commitment.

In this dream, a twenty-five-year-old woman discovers her father, loaded with chains, and confined in a dungeon. He is calling out piteously for help as she watches through the grille of the closed door, quite immobilised by her fear and helplessness.

Her actual father had become increasingly disabled with arthritis over a period of fifteen years, and was now heavily dependent on his wife and daughter's care. At the time of the dream, the young woman was preoccupied with her own impending marriage, a prospect that was complicated by mixed feelings towards settling down, and by her conflicts about the duties and obligations she felt surrounding her parents' situation.

Clearly, the misfortunes of her own parents could be seen as a dire warning of what might happen if she committed herself in a long-term partnership: any one of us might reasonably fear ending up in a similar situation, chained and imprisoned by a partner who becomes totally dependent on us through illness.

Your experience with the Dream Lover should by now allow you to take a wider perspective, beyond the purely real-life aspects of such a dream, so let us consider this image in somewhat broader terms. Here is the Dream Lover as The Chained Man, representing the dreamer's opposite in every way, for *she* is a woman, young, healthy and free.

His challenge to her is, 'Unchain me!', and , *since he is part of herself,* 'Unchain yourself from your fears of dependency within marriage.' And the further message for this dreamer could be, 'Remember, *your* life is not your mother's life, *your* partner will not be your father, although your unconscious fears and hesitations arise from that source. You can take the risk of moving on from the young-and-single role.' Here, once again, the Dream Lover chooses a dramatic and emotionally stirring image to spur the dreamer into considering the need to change and grow.

The Parent Role

The parenting role, the reproduction of our species, is the biological foundation and the primary function of the gender division. Regardless of whatever we may think or do about it, regardless of the circumstances or the consequences, Nature — or at least *our* natures — will always find a way to obey the over-riding imperative to continue the race.

But having acknowledged the powerful and compelling forces prompting us to become a mother or father, these are still largely roles of personal choice. This is especially true in contemporary western societies, where the reproductive process can be readily prevented, aborted or deferred, and where the automatic assumption that a couple only exists to raise a family is itself being radically reassessed.

In this short space, I will not attempt to discuss the wide variety of opinions and theories about why, when or whether we should become parents, nor how we should raise our children. I want instead to touch upon just a few of the issues that can arise when a couple enter into parenthood, the effects of these roles upon personal development, and ways in which we can become stuck in these roles:

— Parenthood can be, and often is, entered into through unconscious choice or 'accident'. It can be a blind effort to escape or cover up other important issues. Teenagers may

180

unconsciously hope to find a short-cut to adulthood by becoming pregnant; adult couples may wish to blur existing difficulties within a relationship, or to cement a dubious partnership, by having a child. Others may choose parenthood as a means of achieving a role of power, control, status, or self-esteem, having failed to find these satisfactions in other areas of their lives. However, issues that are avoided in this way are unlikely to be resolved but are simply deferred to cause problems later.

— Parenthood inevitably re-stimulates powerful gender 'recordings' received from one's own parents, under the general heading of 'How to be a proper Mother or Father'. No matter how strongly we may resist repeating our parents' mistakes and shortcomings, there is a built-in tendency to revert to the rules learned unconsciously in early years, especially in times of stress. When two people carry seriously conflicting programmes about how to be a parent (strict or permissive, distant or closely involved, etc.), the arrival of the first child can become a focus for many new relationship difficulties.

— Parenthood may also trigger off unresolved problems of deprivation or dependency, in either partner. As a result, the relationship may be soured by unconscious feelings of jealousy towards the baby, who is felt to be a rival for the spouse's love and attention (see Chapter 11).

— Parenthood is a long-term role, at least twenty years. Thus, it severely tests our attitudes about personal freedom, loyalty and duty within the role. How will we balance our feelings of frustration and boredom with this long-term responsibility?

— Parenthood can be marvellously fulfilling, a role that satisfies all our deepest needs. Becoming a father or mother may feel like the achievement of an ultimate, complete personal and gender identity. Yet, will it be possible to stay in this role, refusing all further changes, for the rest of our lives? The Good Mother and the Good Father are a pair of gender roles that are totally endorsed and admired by society, that are important, benevolent and personally rewarding. But *because* of this they invite over-identification and role fixation, making it especially difficult to grow out of them and eventually move on.

This last point becomes increasingly important in midlife, the subject of the next section, but first I would like to add some notes on the role of the Dream Lover within the complex and shifting relationship patterns to be found between couples with children.

If the central issue during the teenage transition is 'Child identity versus Adult identity', and the key debate for young single people is 'Freedom versus Commitment', then many of the dilemmas of parenthood stem from the conflict between our ideas about 'Selfishness versus Self-sacrifice'. The average dutiful mother or father, immersed in the stressful responsibilities of parenthood might frequently wonder, 'What about *me*?' but any such thoughts are promptly countered by the equally important question, 'What about the children?' In a healthy and intimate relationship, the partners will be able to raise and discuss these feelings, and seek ways to accommodate the conflict. There are encouraging signs that new ways are being worked out to share the many duties of parenting more widely. Significantly, part of this process is increased role-swapping, softening and breaking up the traditional rigid division between 'mother — nurturer' and 'father — breadwinner'.

If you are raising children in a long-term relationship you will be familiar with this dilemma, this constant background tension between personal needs and the needs of the children, which is also likely to provide one of the main themes of your work with the Dream Lover.

In this situation, one role of the Dream Lover is to bring unconscious wishes and fears closer to the surface where they can be more easily dealt with. Your inner opposite will oppose your conscious concepts by focusing your attention on what is going on below the conscious level of your relationship. It may use bizarre, cruel, mocking or seductive images to present the alternative point of view. The 'good mother' might be horrified to dream of herself dallying with young men on a sun-drenched beach, having forgotten, mislaid, or abandoned her children. Yet such a dream may prompt her to consider more seriously whether her own needs are being adequately acknowledged and dealt with, aside from her motherly duties.

Let me end with another example of how the Dream Lover can highlight, through exaggeration, the hidden fears and wishes which lurk below the surface of most 'married with children' relationships. This couple, in their late thirties, with two teenaged children, are unquestionably devoted to their children, and to each other. Yet, after fifteen years in the parent role it would be surprising if they did not occasionally look back with nostalgia to their former status — young, single, childless and *free*!

The husband had been shocked by a dream in which, backing up a van at work, he had *accidentally* run over his wife. Shortly after this, in a dream of her own, the wife was embarrassed to find herself meeting an attractive male friend who persuaded her, *much against her will*, back to his flat and into a classic seduction scene.

In the context of their real-life situation, both these dreams can be seen for what they are — over-dramatised reflections by the Dream Lover of their mutual wishful fantasies of release and freedom from irksome marital duties. At the time, the husband was obliged to do a temporary job he hated, to support his family, and it was in this work setting that he accidentally 'got rid of' his wife, and all the responsibilities she represented.

It was not long before they both found more constructive ways to increase their sense of freedom within their marriage; he, by starting a home-based business where he could devote more time to his real interest in music; she, by finding a job with a local TV station, which gave her more time away from the family, and also added a degree of glamour and excitement to her life.

In Mid-life

The mid-life years (forties and fifties) present new challenges to one's sense of identity and self-worth. Like the teenage transition, this period of change is widely understood as a time of personal crisis; again, it becomes clear that we must learn to give up or grow out of certain life roles and rebalance our personalities on a new level, ready for the next phase of life. However, unlike the adolescent, the man or woman in mid-life often has no clear picture of what the next phase is to be.

As the primary well-defined sexual roles of the mating game and parenting begin to recede, a vacuum is created, and the future can look not so much uncertain as empty. Both men and women can become deeply depressed at this time, as they sense the approaching loss of roles that have formed the major long-term focus for their sense of identity and worth. Traditionally (and still generally), these are: for the man, the end of his work in the world and his role as head of the family; for the woman, the end of her work in the home and her mothering role.

Those who have invested too heavily and exclusively in this central sexual division — the woman who has no interests or capacities outside the home, the man who has centred his whole life around his career — will have most difficulty in letting go of these stereotyped positions during the transition through mid-life.

The damage caused by this uneven pattern of development in the past, the relative immaturity of the inner other half that was neglected, must now be dealt with, if we are to restore our balance and move on. A large part of the task is that many people in mid-life are still seriously hampered by their own unwillingness to become ex-parents.

Well into their sixties, we still find men and women struggling to maintain their rights: as mothers, to tell their daughters how to run their homes and raise their children; as fathers, to instruct their sons on how to run their businesses and handle their families.

Consciously, they are motivated by their natural, unremitting concern and care for 'the children'; children, by the way, who are now independent adults in their thirties and forties. Unconsciously, I fear, the struggle is to maintain a role, an identity as a parent which they feel is *all they have in life*, all they are capable of being, all that stands between them and what they see as the emptiness of their lives in the years ahead.

There is, in our culture, a shortage of positive models or roles to aspire to after mid-life, and one important project for frustrated and unfulfilled ex-parents could be to invent new roles to match these new times. The need is for many positions of respect and value in society, which enable men and women in their fifties, sixties and beyond, to share their harvest of experience, wisdom and developed talents more widely.

Ancient archetypal models for such roles include Sage, Guru, Wise Man, Wise Woman, High Priestess — images which, significantly, are sometimes adopted by the Dream Lover during this life stage. Perhaps some partial modern equivalents can be found in the fields of politics, religion, education, and various relatively new counselling roles and caring agencies.

Balancing Opposites

In mid-life, the challenge to become your own opposite is more pressing, perhaps, than ever before. From being a person with a strong definite gender role and an established secure identity in life, we can find ourselves in crisis, facing emptiness, endings, lack of meaning, and feeling profoundly disturbed, lost, or unbalanced.

A state of unbalance means that there is too much of one thing or not enough of its opposite, which exactly describes the psychological consequence of long-term neglect of one's inner other half. In mid-life, as at all other times of crisis, we are temporarily unbalanced because we are becoming different from what we were before, but this *needs* to happen, if any further development is to take place.

Look again at the above list of positive roles we might aspire to, after the mid-life transition. They are not roles that can be convincingly filled by lop-sided personalities. They are all roles that require balance as a basic qualification: men would need to learn to be receptive and responsive, to temper their traditional authority with emotional empathy; women would need to develop their assertiveness and public presence, to temper their traditional modesty with strongly expressed conviction.

This opposite that we require to rebalance ourselves is often perceived as belonging to the opposite sex, and our sense of identity may initially feel threatened by any move to become that opposite. By including some aspects of our other halves we lose nothing, and could gain immensely in personal growth.

We have already seen several examples of typical images used by the Dream Lover in relation to people in mid-life: themes of death, decay, wasted sterile landscapes, birth, youth, idealisation, are all quite common. I want now to present two dreams of a different nature, in which figures of ambiguous gender are seen. Sometimes a dreamer will actually see the Dream Lover undergo a magic transformation from male to female or vice versa, as in the first dream below.

I have never come across examples of these 'cross-over' dreams in people under forty but I'm sure they do occur at other ages. They seem to belong naturally to the mid-life developmental process of integrating more of the other half.

I will add no comments, for the dreams speak for themselves in the context of what has been said about mid-life rebalancing:

The huge figure of a man dressed in sheepskins threatened to take my new baby from me. I struggled, and as I did so he turned into a giant polar bear. I was powerless to prevent him as he picked up my baby. Then I was amazed to see that the bear had breasts; he began to feed the baby, nursing it at the breast like a woman. I felt anxious and happy at the same time . . . (Dreamed by a forty-two-year-old woman)

A woman, all dressed in red, is dancing rapidly before me. Because she's moving in a blur, I can't quite see who it is; she has red hair, it could be one of several women I've known with red hair. Her whole body, and especially her face, seems to flicker and change continuously — she looks fat, then thin, young, then old. 'You keep changing,' I say out loud, whereupon she stops, and turns to face me. I don't know her. She is extremely pale, with dark-red upswept hair. She wears a sun-visor. Her whole chest is exposed to the waist. She has no breasts but has three sets of flat pink vestigial nipples, like a man's. 'An androgyne,' I hear myself say. (Dreamed by a forty-nine-year-old man. Note: 'androgyne' means 'male and female', a person combining both sexes.)

The Next Chapter

I hope you have enjoyed meeting your Dream Lover through reading this book. It will be clear by now that when you work on your relationships through the Dream Lover, you are working on yourself. The whole purpose of this work is to explore, understand and reclaim more of your own hidden truth, using as a starting point the reflection of yourself as seen in the mirror of your opposite sex dreams.

Reclaiming the psychological territory which is locked up in the illusion that certain aspects of personality belong exclusively to the opposite sex, is a major life task for us all, at any age, and this process is strongly facilitated through dreamwork focused on the Dream Lover.

Paradoxically, the surest route to better relationships is to turn our search for wholeness, for a soul mate, inwards; it is the person who has spent time on this inner exploration and who is comfortable with his or her inner complexity, who will make the easiest companion, the most appreciative lover and the truest partner.

Whatever stage of life you now find yourself in, and whatever the state of your current relationships, you can turn to your inner mirror at any time. Your Dream Lover is always there, waiting to lead you on . . . into the next chapter of your own story.

APPENDIX: FURTHER READING

Dreamwork and Symbolism

Faraday, Ann, *Dream Power*, Berkeley, 1972
Fromm, Erich, *The Forgotten Language*, Grove Press, 1951
Garfield, Patricia, *Creative Dreaming*, Futura, 1976
Jung, Carl G., *Dreams*, Ark, 1985
Jung, Carl G., (ed.), *Man And His Symbols*, Picador, 1978
Shohet, Robin, *Dream Sharing*, Thorsons, 1985

Gender Identity

Arcana, Judith, *Every Mother's Son*, Women's Press, 1983
Arcana, Judith, *Our Mothers' Daughters*, Women's Press, 1981
Dickson, Anne, *The Mirror Within*, Quartet, 1985
Forisha, Barbara, *Sex Roles and Personal Awareness*, General Learning Press, 1978
Friday, Nancy, *My Mother, My Self*, Fontana, 1979
Johnson, Robert, *He*, Perennial Library, 1977
Johnson, Robert, *She*, Perennial Library, 1977
Korda, Michael, *Male Chauvinism*, Barrie & Jenkins, 1974

Psychology and Interpersonal Relationships

Argyle, Michael, *The Psychology Of Interpersonal Behaviour*, Pelican, 1967

Berne, Eric, *Games People Play*, Penguin, 1968

Dickson, Anne, *A Woman In Your Own Right*, Quartet, 1982

Dominian, Jack, *Marital Breakdown*, Penguin, 1968

Harris, Thomas, *I'm OK, You're OK*, Pan, 1973

Personal Development

Ernst, Sheila, and Goodison, Lucy, *In Our Own Hands*, Women's Press, 1981 (A very good introduction to many of the humanistic techniques used in self-help groups, led groups, and individual therapy.)

Human Potential Magazine, 5 Layton Road, London N1 OPX (A quarterly magazine carrying articles on humanistic psychology and related subjects, plus a directory of groups, courses and organisations.)

Resource Centres

Readers interested in further personal development work, including the use of dreams and guided imagery, can write to the following organisations for information about groups, courses, training, and individual practitioners in their own areas:

The Association of Humanistic Psychology Practitioners (AHPP), General Secretary, 45 Litchfield Way, London NW11 6NU

The Psychosynthesis And Education Trust, 188–194 Old Street, London EC1V 9BP

The Transpersonal Psychology Study Centre, 7 Pembridge Place, London W2 4XB

INDEX

encouragement of dreams, 33
expectations
  v. experience, 76

families
  and development of gender
    identity, 120–3
  gender alliances within, 123
fear, 86–8

gender alliances
  within families, 123
gender identity, 115–6
  influence of family on
    development of, 120–3
  influence of parents on
    development of, 117–20
gender role
  assumptions about, 115–6
  fixation in , 173–4, 181
  self within the, 129–39

healing
  dreams and, 162–3
helplessness
  and fear, 87

idealisation
  of the opposite sex, 74–81
imagination
  and dealing with jealousy,
    101–2
independence
  development of, 137–9, 174
interpretation of dreams
  cultural context, 23–4
  personal context, 24–6
introjection, 133–5

jealousy

and childhood experience, 97
and dependency, 100
and deprivation, 99–100
dreams about, 96–102
towards children, 182
Jung, Carl Gustav, 7, 13

mid-life, 184–5

nightmares
  dealing with, 94–5
  Dream Lover in, 85–6

opposite
  becoming your own, 172–3
  inner, 12–13
opposites, balancing of, 185–7

parent–child relationship
  and dependency, 100
  and deprivation, 99
  and development of gender
    identity, 117–20
  and idealisation of opposite
    sex, 77
  and introjection, 133–5
  questionnaires on, 117–120
  and retroflection, 136
parenthood, 180–4
  effect on relationships, 182
  and gender role fixation, 182
  and personal needs of
    parents, 183–4
Perfect Partner figure, see
  idealisation
pheromones, 42
pictures in dreams, 19–21
potential
  development of, 52–4
problem-solving

191